Quesadilla Cookbook

Delicious Quesadilla Recipes for All
Types of Tasty Quesadillas

By
BookSumo Press

Published by
http://www.booksumo.com

Table of Contents

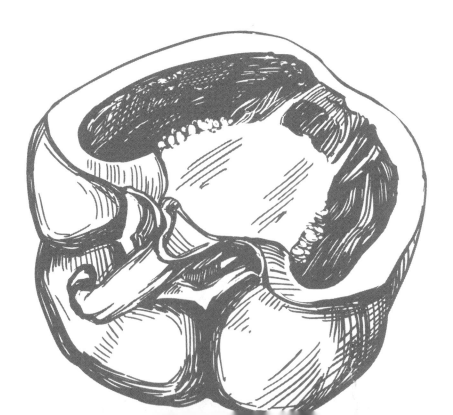

Napa Valley
Topped Avocado Quesadillas

Prep Time: 35 mins
Total Time: 45 mins

Servings per Recipe: 4
Calories   382.2
Fat   17.3g
Cholesterol   0.0mg
Sodium   574.1mg
Carbohydrates   49.8g
Protein   8.3g

Ingredients

1 avocado, peeled and pitted
2 tsp lime juice
1 tsp minced garlic
1/8 C. chopped green onion
1/4 C. diced tomato
1/8 C. diced yellow onion
1/8 C. diced green bell pepper

salt and chili powder
1 tbsp olive oil
48 inches flour tortillas
1 C. shredded cheddar cheese

Directions

1. For the guacamole: in a bowl, add the avocado and lime juice and with a fork, mash it.
2. Add the tomato, bell pepper, green onion, yellow onion, garlic, salt and chili powder and stir to combine well.
3. Cover the bowl and place in the fridge for about 25-30 minutes.
4. In a skillet, add the oil over medium heat and cook until heated.
5. Put 1 tortilla and top with about 1/3 C. of the cheese.
6. Cook until cheese melts and then top with some of the guacamole.
7. Cover with another tortilla and carefully, flip the quesadilla.
8. Cook until the tortilla becomes golden brown.
9. Transfer the quesadilla onto a plate.
10. Repeat with the remaining tortillas, cheese and guacamole.
11. Cut each quesadilla into wedges and enjoy.

WACO
Chicken Quesadillas

 Prep Time: 5 mins
Total Time: 10 mins

Servings per Recipe: 2
Calories   414.8
Fat   28.1g
Cholesterol   22.1mg
Sodium   859.7mg
Carbohydrates   32.9g
Protein   7.3g

Ingredients
4 flour tortillas
1/4 C. chicken, shredded and seasoned with
fajita seasoning
1/4 C. turkey bacon, cooked and crumbled
4 tbsp ranch dressing
red pepper flakes
Monterey jack cheese

Directions
1. Place 2 tbsp of the ranch dressing onto 2 tortillas evenly and top with the cheese, followed by the chicken and bacon.
2. Sprinkle with the red pepper flakes and cover each with the remaining tortillas.
3. Place a greased pan over heat until heated through.
4. Add the quesadillas and cook for about 2-4 minutes, flipping once half way through.

Camping
Breakfast Quesadillas

🥣 Prep Time: 15 mins
🕐 Total Time: 25 mins

Servings per Recipe: 6
Calories	240.4
Fat	14.8g
Cholesterol	104.0mg
Sodium	374.6mg
Carbohydrates	12.9g
Protein	13.3g

Ingredients
20 inches flour tortillas
2 C. Monterey jack cheese, shredded
2 eggs, scrambled
1/2 C. beef sausage, cooked, crumbled
1/4 C. green onion, diced
1/4 C. tomatoes, diced
guacamole

sour cream
salsa

Directions
1. Place a skillet over heat and cook until heated completely.
2. Place both tortillas and top with the cheese evenly.
3. Place the scrambled eggs onto 1 tortilla, followed by the sausage and cook until cheese is melted.
4. Now, place the tomatoes over sausage, followed by the green onions.
5. Cover with the second tortilla, cheese side down.
6. Transfer the quesadilla onto a platter.
7. Cut into 6 equal sized wedges and enjoy alongside the salsa, guacamole and sour cream.

GERMAN
Dessert
Quesadillas

 Prep Time: 5 mins
Total Time: 10 mins

Servings per Recipe: 4
Calories   333.2
Fat   22.1g
Cholesterol   38.4mg
Sodium   303.0mg
Carbohydrates   31.5g
Protein   5.6g

Ingredients
1/4 C. butter
4 small flour tortillas
1/2 C. semi-sweet chocolate chips
ground cinnamon
sugar
1 C. vanilla yogurt

Directions
1. Place a thin layer of the butter onto both sides of all tortillas.
2. Place a skillet over medium-high heat and until heated.
3. Place the tortillas and top each with the chocolate chips, followed by the sugar and cinnamon.
4. Cook until the chocolate just begins to melt.
5. Carefully, fold each tortilla and cook until golden brown from both sides.
6. Cut into wedges and enjoy alongside the vanilla yogurt.

Chopped
Chicken Quesadillas

Prep Time: 5 mins
Total Time: 18 mins

Servings per Recipe: 2
Calories	1301.8
Fat	53.9g
Cholesterol	170.5mg
Sodium	3626.0mg
Carbohydrates	132.9g
Protein	69.2g

Ingredients

8 (8 inch) flour tortillas
1 (4 oz.) cans chopped mild green chilies
2 C. shredded and chopped rotisserie-cooked chicken
1/2 C. shredded extra-sharp cheddar cheese
1/2 C. bottled taco sauce

cilantro stem
1 C. bottled salsa
1/4 C. sour cream

Directions

1. Set your oven to 450 degrees F before doing anything else.
2. In the bottom of a baking sheet, arrange 4 tortillas and top each with the chilies, followed by the chicken, cheese and taco sauce.
3. Cover with the remaining tortillas.
4. Cook in the oven for about 8 minutes.
5. Remove from the oven and keep aside for about 5 minutes.
6. Cut into quarters and enjoy with a topping of the salsa, cilantro and sour cream.

FRIENDSHIP
Quesadillas

Prep Time: 10 mins
Total Time: 12 mins

Servings per Recipe: 4
Calories   385.8
Fat   15.5g
Cholesterol   22.4mg
Sodium   1328.3mg
Carbohydrates   48.2g
Protein   14.0g

Ingredients
1 tbsp canola oil
2 C. red onions, chopped
1/2 tsp sugar
4 C. spinach leaves
4 burrito-size flour tortillas
4 oz. grated mozzarella cheese
1 (7 oz.) jars roasted red peppers, drained,
rinsed and cut into strips

Directions
1. In a skillet, add the oil over medium heat and cook until heated through.
2. Add the onions and stir fry for about 4 minutes.
3. Add the sugar and cook for about 9-10 minutes.
4. Stir in the spinach and immediately, remove from the heat.
5. Place another skilled over medium-high heat until heated through.
6. Place 1 tortilla and cook for about 15 seconds.
7. Place 1/2 C. of the cheese onto half of the tortilla, followed by 1/4 of the spinach mixture and 1/4 of the pepper strips.
8. Fold the tortilla over the filling and cook for about 10 seconds, pressing with the spatula.
9. Transfer the quesadilla onto a platter.
10. Repeat with the remaining tortillas and filling ingredients.
11. Enjoy warm.

Alaskan Kale
Quesadillas

🥣 Prep Time: 5 mins
🕐 Total Time: 20 mins

Servings per Recipe: 4
Calories   110.5
Fat   5.4g
Cholesterol   37.8mg
Sodium   699.3mg
Carbohydrates   1.9g
Protein   13.8g

Ingredients

2 tsp extra virgin olive oil
1 C. kale, stems removed, shredded
1 tsp kosher salt
1/2 C. shredded low-fat cheddar cheese
1/2 C. shredded Asiago cheese
32 inches whole wheat tortillas
6 oz. canned pink salmon, flaked

Directions

1. In a nonstick skillet, add 1 tsp of the oil over medium heat and cook until heated through.
2. Add the kale and cook for about 5 minutes.
3. Stir in the salt and transfer the kale into a bowl.
4. In a bowl, add all the cheeses and mix well.
5. In the same skillet, add the remaining oil over medium heat and cook until heated through.
6. Place 1 tortilla and top with 1/4 C. of the kale, followed by 1/4 of the salmon and 1/4 C. of the cheese mixture.
7. Fold the tortilla over the filling and cook for about 2 minutes, flipping once half way through, pressing lightly with the back of a spatula.
8. Repeat with the remaining tortillas and filling.
9. Cut each quesadilla into triangles and enjoy.

AMERICAN
Chicken
Quesadillas

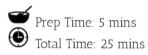
Prep Time: 5 mins
Total Time: 25 mins

Servings per Recipe: 5

Calories	454.0
Fat	23.8g
Cholesterol	90.0mg
Sodium	1447.5mg
Carbohydrates	31.0g
Protein	29.7g

Ingredients

1 lb. chicken breasts, cut into pieces
1 (28 oz.) cans crushed tomatoes
2 C. chicken broth
1 (8 oz.) jars salsa
5 canned jalapeño slices, chopped
1 1/2 - 2 tsp cumin
1/2 tsp garlic powder
salt
5 - 6 flour tortillas

5 - 6 slices white American cheese
3 tbsp butter

Directions

1. In a pan, add the salsa, tomatoes, jalapeños, garlic, cumin, salt and broth and cook until boiling.
2. Add the chicken and stir to combine well.
3. Set the heat to medium-low and cook until chicken is done completely.
4. With a slotted spoon, transfer the chicken pieces onto a plate.
5. Place the cheese in the center of each tortilla, followed by the chicken pieces.
6. Fold the tortillas around the filling.
7. In a pot, add 1/2 tbsp of the butter over medium-low heat.
8. Cook for about 2 minutes, flipping once half way through.
9. Enjoy warm.

Tropical
Chicken Quesadillas

🥣 Prep Time: 10 mins
🕐 Total Time: 25 mins

Servings per Recipe: 8
Calories	451.1
Fat	19.1g
Cholesterol	58.1mg
Sodium	723.6mg
Carbohydrates	46.5g
Protein	22.2g

Ingredients

1/4 C. honey mustard
2 tbsp pineapple preserves
8 (10 inch) flour tortillas
1 1/2 C. shredded Swiss cheese
2 tbsp butter
2 C. chopped cooked chicken
1/2 C. crumbled cooked turkey bacon

1 1/2 C. unsweetened pineapple tidbits, drained

Directions

1. In a bowl, add the pineapple preserves and mustard and mix well.
2. Place the mustard mixture in the center of 4 of the tortillas evenly, followed by the Swiss cheese, chicken and bacon.
3. Cover with the remaining tortillas.
4. In a skillet, add a little butter over medium heat and cook until melted.
5. Place 1 quesadilla and cook for about 3 minutes, flipping once half way through.
6. Repeat with the remaining quesadillas.
7. Enjoy warm with a topping of the pineapple tidbits.

MID-SUMMER
Ranch Quesadillas

Prep Time: 10 mins
Total Time: 16 mins

Servings per Recipe: 6
Calories	381.5
Fat	18.2g
Cholesterol	46.9mg
Sodium	903.7mg
Carbohydrates	35.4g
Protein	21.1g

Ingredients
6 whole wheat tortillas
1 avocado, sliced
1 C. shredded cooked chicken
2 C. mozzarella cheese, shredded
1 C. reduced-fat cheddar cheese, shredded
1 1/2 C. portabella mushrooms, sliced
1 C. sun-dried tomato, julienned
1/2 C. green onion, chopped
cooking spray

light ranch salad dressing
salsa

Directions
1. Place the avocado slices onto one half of each tortilla, followed by the chicken, mozzarella cheese, cheddar cheese, mushrooms, sun-dried tomato and green onion.
2. Fold each tortilla over the filling and press slightly.
3. Grease a skillet with the cooking spray slightly and place over medium-low heat until heated through.
4. Place 1 quesadilla and cook for about 4-6 minutes, flipping once half way through.
5. Repeat with the remaining quesadillas.
6. Cut each quesadilla into 3 wedges and enjoy alongside the salsa and ranch dressing.

Hot
Mushroom Quesadillas

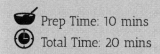 Prep Time: 10 mins

Total Time: 20 mins

Servings per Recipe: 4
Calories	518.2
Fat	28.5g
Cholesterol	42.8mg
Sodium	1107.7mg
Carbohydrates	47.6g
Protein	19.4g

Ingredients

1 tbsp olive oil
1 garlic clove, minced
1 medium onion, chopped
1/4 C. diced bell pepper
12 oz. white mushrooms, sliced
2 jalapeño peppers, seeded and chopped
1/2 tsp salt

1/4 tsp pepper
1/3 C. mayonnaise
4 burrito-size flour tortillas
1 1/2 C. shredded Monterey jack cheese

Directions

1. In a skillet, add the oil over medium-high heat and cook until heated.
2. Add the mushrooms, bell peppers, onion, garlic, jalapeños, salt and pepper and cook for about 8-10 minutes, mixing often.
3. Remove from the heat and place the vegetable mixture into a bowl.
4. Keep aside to cool.
5. After cooling, add the mayonnaise and mix well.
6. Arrange the tortillas onto a platter.
7. Place the cheese onto each tortilla, followed by the mushroom mixture.
8. Fold each tortilla in half.
9. Place a nonstick skillet over medium heat until heated through.
10. Place the quesadillas in batches and cook for about 2-4 minutes, flipping once half way through.
11. Enjoy warm.

SOUTHWEST
Yam Quesadillas

Prep Time: 30 mins
Total Time: 40 mins

Servings per Recipe: 4
Calories	700.6
Fat	28.7g
Cholesterol	29.6mg
Sodium	976.4mg
Carbohydrates	91.6g
Protein	19.4g

Ingredients
1 1/2 C. chopped onions
2 garlic cloves, minced
3 tbsp vegetable oil
4 C. grated peeled sweet potatoes
1/2 tsp dried oregano
1 tsp chili powder
2 tsp ground cumin
1 - 2 pinch cayenne
salt and pepper

1 C. shredded sharp cheddar cheese
8 (8 inch) flour tortillas
salsa
sour cream

Directions
1. In a nonstick skillet, add the oil and cook until heated through.
2. Add the onions and garlic and stir fry for about 3-4 minutes.
3. Stir in the oregano, sweet potatoes, cumin, chili powder and cayenne and cook, covered for about 9-10 minutes, mixing frequently.
4. Stir in the salt and pepper and remove from the heat.
5. Place the sweet potato mixture onto each tortilla evenly, followed by the cheese.
6. Fold each tortilla in half.
7. Place a greased nonstick skillet over medium-high heat until heated through.
8. Place the quesadillas in batches and cook for about 4-6 minutes, flipping once half way through.
9. Enjoy alongside the salsa and sour cream.

Roasted
Quesadillas for Sunday

🥣 Prep Time: 10 mins
🕐 Total Time: 40 mins

Servings per Recipe: 4
Calories   521.6
Fat   15.8g
Cholesterol   73.0mg
Sodium   1022.9mg
Carbohydrates   57.5g
Protein   35.0g

Ingredients
6 tortillas
2 C. chopped cooked boneless skinless
chicken breasts
1/4 C. chopped green onion
1/4 C. chopped tomato
3/4 C. shredded cheese, cheddar
1/4 C. salsa

Directions
1. Set your oven to 425 degrees F before doing anything else and lightly, grease a baking sheet.
2. In a bowl, add the cheese, chicken, vegetables and salsa and mix well.
3. In the bottom of a baking sheet, arrange 2 tortillas and top each with 1/4 of the chicken mixture.
4. Repeat the layers with the remaining tortillas and chicken mixture, pressing down slightly.
5. With a piece of the foil, cover the top tortilla loosely.
6. Cook in the oven for about 20 minutes.
7. Cut each quesadilla into 6 wedges and enjoy.
8. Another option: place chicken mixture onto all tortillas evenly.
9. Roll each tortilla over the filling.
10. In the bottom of a baking sheet, arrange the quesadillas, seam side down.
11. Cook in the oven for the same temperature and cooking time as mentioned above.

CENTRAL PARK
Hot Dog Quesadillas

Prep Time: 10 mins
Total Time: 30 mins

Servings per Recipe: 4
Calories	488.4
Fat	31.8g
Cholesterol	61.8mg
Sodium	1614.3mg
Carbohydrates	32.1g
Protein	19.7g

Ingredients
2 tsp olive oil, divided
4 kosher hot dogs, cut into slivers
4 flour tortillas
1 C. chili
1/4 C. ketchup
1 1/2 C. shredded cheese

Directions
1. In a skillet, add 1 tsp of the oil over medium heat and cook until heated through.
2. Add the hot dog slivers and cook until browned completely.
3. With a slotted spoon, place the hot dog slivers into a bowl and keep aside.
4. Place the chili over one half of each tortilla, followed by the hot dog slivers, ketchup, and 1/3 C. of cheese.
5. Fold the tortilla over the filling.
6. In the same skillet, add the remaining oil and cook until heated through.
7. Add 1 quesadilla and cook until golden brown from both sides.
8. Repeat with the remaining quesadillas.
9. Enjoy warm.

Quesadilla
Festival

Prep Time: 20 mins
Total Time: 30 mins

Servings per Recipe: 4
Calories	224.7
Fat	6.8g
Cholesterol	18.3mg
Sodium	173.8mg
Carbohydrates	26.2g
Protein	16.2g

Ingredients

Salsa
1/2 C. chopped tomato
3 tbsp chopped red onions
1 tsp minced jalapeño
3 tbsp diced red bell peppers
1 tsp chopped cilantro leaves
1 tbsp lime juice
salt
ground pepper
Quesadilla
1 (15 oz.) cans black beans, rinsed and drained

2 tbsp chopped fresh cilantro leaves
3/4 C. chopped red onion
3/4 C. chopped tomato
1 garlic clove, minced
1/4 tsp ground cumin
1/2 tsp adobo seasoning
salt
fresh ground pepper
4 large whole wheat tortillas
1 C. low-fat Monterey jack cheese
nonfat sour cream

Directions

1. For the salsa: in a bowl, add all the ingredients and mix well.
2. Place in the fridge until using.
3. In another bowl, add the beans, tomatoes, onions, garlic, cilantro, adobo, cumin, salt and pepper and toss to coat well.
4. Place about 1/8 of the cheese onto one half of each tortilla, followed by 1/4 of the beans mixture and 1/8 of the cheese.
5. Fold each tortilla in half over the filling.
6. Place a nonstick skillet over medium heat until heated through.
7. Place 1 quesadilla and cook until golden brown from both sides.
8. Repeat with the remaining quesadillas.
9. Cut each quesadilla into 4 wedges and enjoy hot with a topping of the salsa and sour cream.

LOS ANGELES
Corn Quesadillas

🥣 Prep Time: 20 mins
🕐 Total Time: 40 mins

Servings per Recipe: 1
Calories	605.5
Fat	21.8g
Cholesterol	34.6mg
Sodium	1033.0mg
Carbohydrates	84.2g
Protein	21.5g

Ingredients

1/2 tbsp olive oil
2 C. corn kernels
1/4 tsp salt
1 pinch ground black pepper
1 scallion, sliced on diagonal
1/4 C. water
oil, for pan
6 large flour tortillas
1 1/2 C. white cheddar cheese, grated

1/3 C. cilantro, chopped
3 roasted poblano chilies, diced
Toppings
guacamole
Mexican crema
1 sprig cilantro
salsa

Directions

1. In a pot, add the oil over medium heat and cook until heated through.
2. Add the corn, salt and pepper and cook for about 1 minute.
3. Add the water and scallion and cook, covered for about 4 minutes.
4. Remove from the heat and place the corn mixture into a bowl.
5. Place a greased cast-iron skillet over heat until heated through.
6. Place the tortillas, 1 at a time and cook for about 30 seconds per side.
7. Place about 1/3 C. of the corn mixture on half of each tortilla, followed by the cheese, cilantro and diced chilies.
8. Fold each tortilla over the filling.
9. Place a greased skillet over medium-low heat until heated through.
10. Place the quesadillas in batches and cook until golden brown from both sides.
11. Cut each quesadilla into wedges and enjoy with a garnishing of the guacamole, crema, salsa and cilantro.

Japanese
Sirloin Quesadillas

🥄 Prep Time: 20 mins

🕐 Total Time: 35 mins

Servings per Recipe: 18
Calories	104.6
Fat	4.8g
Cholesterol	16.1mg
Sodium	379.0mg
Carbohydrates	7.7g
Protein	7.3g

Ingredients

1/3 C. reduced sodium soy sauce
1/3 C. reduced-sodium chicken broth
1 tbsp brown sugar
1 tsp minced gingerroot
1/2 tsp onion powder
1 garlic clove, minced
1 lb. beef top sirloin steak

1/2 C. chopped fresh pineapple
1/2 C. chopped red onion
1/2 C. chopped green pepper
2 C. shredded part-skim mozzarella cheese
6 flour tortillas

Directions

1. In a bowl, add the ginger, garlic, soy sauce, broth and brown sugar and mix well.
2. In a bowl, 3 tbsp of the ginger mixture and preserve for the filling.
3. In a zip lock bag, add the remaining ginger mixture into and steak.
4. Seal the bag and shake to coat well.
5. Place in the fridge for about 2 hours.
6. Set your grill for medium heat and lightly, grease the grill grate.
7. Remove the steak from the bag and discard the marinade.
8. Place the steak onto the grill and cook, covered for about 8-11 minutes per side.
9. Transfer the steak onto a cutting board to cool slightly.
10. With a sharp knife, cut the steak into bite-size pieces.
11. In a bowl, add the beef, pineapple, green pepper and red onion and mix well.
12. Place half of the cheese onto 3 tortillas, followed by the beef mixture, reserved ginger mixture and remaining cheese.
13. Cover with the remaining tortillas.
14. Place the quesadillas onto the grill over medium heat and cook for about 2-4 minutes, flipping once half way trough.
15. Cut each quesadilla into six wedges and enjoy.

HONEY
Chicken
Quesadillas

Prep Time: 15 mins

Total Time: 20 mins

Servings per Recipe: 4

Calories	375.1
Fat	15.9g
Cholesterol	54.7mg
Sodium	598.3mg
Carbohydrates	36.9g
Protein	20.4g

Ingredients
1 tsp honey
1/2 tsp lime juice
1/2 C. reduced-fat sour cream
4 (8 inch) flour tortillas
3/4 C. pepper jack cheese, shredded
1 C. cooked chicken breast
1 C. sliced peeled firm ripe peach
4 tsp chopped cilantro
cooking spray

Directions
1. For the sauce: in a bowl, add the sour cream, lime juice and honey and beat until well combined.
2. Cover the bowl and place in the fridge to chill before using.
3. Place 2 tbsp of the cheese onto half of each tortilla, followed by 1/4 C. of the chicken, 1/4 C. of the peaches, 1 tsp of the cilantro and 1 tbsp of the cheese.
4. Fold each tortilla over the filling in half.
5. Place a greased nonstick skillet over medium-high heat until heated through.
6. Place the quesadillas, 2 at a time in the pan and top with a another heavy skillet for weight.
7. Cook for about 3 minutes, flipping once half way through.
8. Slice each quesadilla into desired sized wedges and enjoy alongside the sauce.

Chopped
Bacon Quesadillas

Prep Time: 30 mins

Total Time: 42 mins

Servings per Recipe: 2

Calories	484.2
Fat	32.8g
Cholesterol	430.0mg
Sodium	857.0mg
Carbohydrates	17.6g
Protein	28.2g

Ingredients

1 tbsp unsalted butter
2 green onions, chopped
4 large eggs, beaten
salt
pepper
4 slices cooked crisp turkey bacon, broken into pieces

2 flour tortillas
1/2 C. shredded Monterey jack cheese
vegetable oil

Directions

1. In a nonstick skillet, add the butter over medium-high heat and cook until melted.
2. Add the onion and stir fry for about 20 seconds.
3. Add the beaten eggs, salt and pepper and cook until just set, mixing frequently.
4. Stir in the bacon and remove from the heat.
5. Place the bacon mixture onto each tortilla evenly, followed by the cheese.
6. Fold each tortilla in half over the filling.
7. Coat the quesadillas with the oil slightly.
8. Place another skillet over medium heat until heated through.
9. Place the quesadillas and cook for about 2 minutes, flipping once half way through.
10. Enjoy hot.

HOT
Turkey Quesadillas

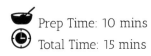

Prep Time: 10 mins
Total Time: 15 mins

Servings per Recipe: 1
Calories	298.7
Fat	16.4g
Cholesterol	61.7mg
Sodium	1226.1mg
Carbohydrates	21.8g
Protein	16.2g

Ingredients
1 flour tortilla
1/3 C. shredded Mexican blend cheese
1 - 2 slice deli turkey, cubed
1 tsp chopped jalapeño
1 - 2 tbsp salsa

Directions
1. Place tortilla into grill pan and place cheese over half the tortilla, followed by the cubed meat and jalapeño.
2. Fold each tortilla in half to cover the filling.
3. Place a greased grill pan over heat until heated through.
4. Place the quesadillas and cook for until golden brown from both sides.
5. Enjoy alongside the salsa.

Tuna Quesadillas

🥣 Prep Time: 5 mins

🕐 Total Time: 8 mins

Servings per Recipe: 2
Calories	632.8
Fat	23.7g
Cholesterol	75.4mg
Sodium	1361.2mg
Carbohydrates	62.7g
Protein	40.1g

Ingredients

1 (5 oz.) cans tuna in water, drained
1 small tomatoes, sliced
2 green onions, chopped
1 C. mozzarella cheese, shredded
1/8 tsp dry mustard
2 large flour tortillas

Directions

1. Place the tuna onto 2 tortillas evenly, followed by the dry mustard, green onions, tomato slices and cheese.
2. Fold each tortilla in half over the filling.
3. Heat a grill pan and cook the quesadillas until golden brown from both sides.
4. Enjoy hot.

NEW HAMPSHIRE
Salmon Quesadillas

Prep Time: 10 mins
Total Time: 20 mins

Servings per Recipe: 4
Calories   556.5
Fat   30.9g
Cholesterol   59.4mg
Sodium   1044.6mg
Carbohydrates   42.1g
Protein   27.5g

Ingredients

1 medium cucumber, peeled, seeded and chopped
1/2 C. salsa
8 oz. salmon fillets
3 tbsp olive oil, divided
40 inches flour tortillas, warmed
6 oz. goat cheese, crumbled
1/4 C. pickled jalapeño pepper, drained and sliced

Directions

1. Set your barbecue grill for medium-high heat and lightly, grease the grill grate.
2. In a bowl, add the salsa and cucumber and mix well.
3. Coat the salmon with 2 tbsp of the oil evenly.
4. Place the salmon onto the grill and cook, covered for about 10-12 minutes, flipping once half way through.
5. Remove from the grill and place the salmon onto a plate.
6. With a fork, flake the salmon.
7. Again, set your barbecue grill for medium-high heat and lightly, grease the grill grate.
8. Place the salmon onto half of each tortilla, leaving 1-inch edges, followed by the cheese and jalapeño pepper.
9. Fold each tortilla in half over the filling.
10. Coat the tortillas with the remaining 1 tbsp of the oil.
11. Cook the quesadillas onto the grill until golden brown from both sides.
12. Enjoy alongside the cucumber salsa.

Dutchess
Whole Wheat Quesadillas

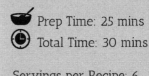 Prep Time: 25 mins

Total Time: 30 mins

Servings per Recipe: 6
Calories	13.4
Fat	0.1g
Cholesterol	0.0mg
Sodium	2.5mg
Carbohydrates	2.4g
Protein	1.3g

Ingredients

vegetable oil cooking spray
8 oz. sliced fresh mushrooms
1/2 medium onion, sliced and separated into rings
1 tsp bottled minced garlic
3 tbsp chopped cilantro
24 inches whole wheat tortillas

6 tbsp shredded low-fat Monterey jack pepper cheese
salsa

Directions

1. Set your oven to 350 degrees F.
2. Grease a skillet with the cooking spray and heat over medium heat.
3. Add the onion, mushrooms and garlic and cook for about 6-7 minutes.
4. Stir in the cilantro and remove from the heat.
5. Place the mushroom mixture on half of each tortilla evenly, followed by the cheese.
6. Fold each tortilla in half over the filling.
7. Arrange the quesadillas onto a baking sheet.
8. Cook in the oven for about 5 minutes.
9. Cut each quesadilla into 4 wedges and enjoy warm.

HOW TO MAKE
a Quesadilla

Prep Time: 10 mins
Total Time: 12 mins

Servings per Recipe: 1

Calories	273.4
Fat	15.3g
Cholesterol	32.8mg
Sodium	896.7mg
Carbohydrates	18.8g
Protein	14.6g

Ingredients
1 soft flour tortilla
1 oz. sliced roasted turkey
3 slices green pickled jalapeño peppers,
sliced rounds, chopped
1/4 C. grated cheese
1 scallion, sliced
3 cilantro leaves
1 tsp olive oil
salsa

Directions
1. Place turkey onto the one side of the tortilla, followed by the pickled jalapeño, cheese, scallion and cilantro leaves.
2. Fold each tortilla in half over the filling.
3. Coat each side of quesadilla with the oil evenly.
4. Place a grill pan over medium-high heat until heated through.
5. Place the quesadilla and cook until golden brown from both sides.
6. Cut the quesadilla into 3 triangles and enjoy.

Chipotle
Quesadillas

🥣 Prep Time: 15 mins

🕐 Total Time: 35 mins

Servings per Recipe: 4

Calories	318.2
Fat	8.9g
Cholesterol	0.0mg
Sodium	540.1mg
Carbohydrates	52.2g
Protein	11.3g

Ingredients
1 zucchini, chopped
1 head broccoli, chopped into florets
1 medium red pepper, chopped
1 medium green pepper, chopped
1 large onion, chopped
2 garlic cloves, minced
1 tomatoes, seeded and chopped

2 tbsp salsa
1 tbsp olive oil
8 flour tortillas
1 C. chipotle cheddar cheese, grated
jalapeño

Directions
1. In a skillet, add 1 tbsp of the olive oil and cook until heated through.
2. Add the vegetables except the tomato and cook for about 5-6 minutes.
3. Add the tomato and cook for about 2 minutes.
4. Add the salsa and cook until heated completely.
5. Place the vegetable mixture onto one side of all the tortillas evenly, followed by the cheese and jalapeños.
6. Fold each tortilla over the filling.
7. Heat a skillet and cook the quesadillas until golden brown from both sides.
8. Enjoy hot.

MARIA'S
Quesadillas de Maiz

 Prep Time: 20 mins

Total Time: 20 mins

Servings per Recipe: 4
Calories   356.1
Fat   18.8g
Cholesterol   40.1mg
Sodium   985.2mg
Carbohydrates   33.8g
Protein   16.3g

Ingredients

1 tbsp vegetable oil
2 tbsp minced onions
1 garlic clove, minced
1 C. corn kernel
4 oz. sliced mushrooms
1/2 tsp salt
2 canned chipotle chilies, minced
2 - 3 tsp adobo sauce
vegetable oil, for frying

8 corn tortillas
6 - 8 oz. Monterey jack cheese, shredded
2 - 3 tbsp minced cilantro
salsa

Directions

1. In a skillet, add 1 tbsp of the oil over medium heat and cook until heated through.

2. Add the onion and garlic and stir fry for about 1 minute.

3. stir in the corn, chipotles, mushrooms and salt and cook for about 5 minutes.

4. Place the vegetable mixture onto 4 tortillas evenly, followed by the cheese and cilantro.

5. Cover with the remaining tortillas.

6. Place a lightly greased heavy-bottomed skillet over medium heat until heated through.

7. Place quesadillas, 1 at a time and cook until golden brown from both sides.

8. Cut each quesadilla into wedges and enjoy alongside the salsa.

Monterey
Poblano Quesadillas

🥣 Prep Time: 15 mins

🕐 Total Time: 25 mins

Servings per Recipe: 6

Calories	712.8
Fat	42.5g
Cholesterol	67.4mg
Sodium	1212.8mg
Carbohydrates	56.4g
Protein	28.3g

Ingredients

3 tbsp vegetable oil
8 tsp vegetable oil
1 1/3 lb. poblano chilies, seeded, sliced
3 tbsp water
3 garlic cloves, minced
1/2 C. cilantro, chopped
8 (9 inch) flour tortillas

1 lb. Monterey jack cheese, grated
8 tbsp salsa, purchased

Directions

1. In a heavy-bottomed skillet, add 3 tbsp of the oil over medium heat and cook until heated through.
2. Stir in the chilies and cook, covered for about 9-10 minutes, mixing often.
3. Add the garlic and stir fry for about 1 minute.
4. Remove from the heat and place the chili mixture into a bowl.
5. Add the cilantro, salt and pepper and stir to combine.
6. In another heavy-bottomed skillet, add 1 tsp of the oil over medium-high heat and cook until heated through.
7. Add 1 tortilla and top with 1/4 of the cheese, followed by 1/4 of the chili mixture and 2 tbsp of the salsa.
8. Cover with 1 of the remaining tortilla and cook for about 1 1/2 minutes, flipping once half way through.
9. Repeat with the remaining tortillas and filling.
10. Cut each quesadilla into 6 wedges and enjoy.

SONOMA
Chicken Quesadillas

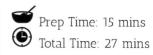

Prep Time: 15 mins
Total Time: 27 mins

Servings per Recipe: 4
Calories   359.1
Fat   18.3g
Cholesterol   30.1mg
Sodium   288.4mg
Carbohydrates   33.8g
Protein   17.8g

Ingredients

8 (6 inch) corn tortillas
6 oz. low-fat Monterey jack cheese
8 oz. smoked chicken breasts, cubed
1 ripe avocado, diced small
1 C. green chili, drained
4 tbsp chopped cilantro leaves
4 oz. nonfat sour cream

Directions

1. Place a cast iron skillet over medium-high heat until heated through.
2. Place 1 tortilla and top with 1/8 of the cheese, followed by 1/4 of the chicken mixture, 1/4 of the avocado, 1/4 of the green chilies, 1/4 of the cilantro and another 1/8 of the cheese.
3. Cover with 1 of the remaining tortilla and cook until golden brown from both sides.
4. Repeat with the remaining tortillas and filling.
5. Cut each quesadilla into 4 pieces and enjoy with a topping of the sour cream.

Quesadillas
Quesadillas

🥣 Prep Time: 15 mins
🕐 Total Time: 25 mins

Servings per Recipe: 4
Calories	342.8
Fat	6.8g
Cholesterol	15.1mg
Sodium	493.1mg
Carbohydrates	67.6g
Protein	6.4g

Ingredients
1/2 C. banana, sliced
1/2 C. strawberry, chopped
1/2 C. mango, chopped
1/2 C. papaya, chopped
4 flour tortillas
1/3 C. Brie cheese, sliced
1 tsp butter

3/4 C. caramel sauce

Directions
1. In a bowl, add the fruit and mix well.
2. In a skillet, add some butter over medium heat and cook until melted.
3. Add 1 tortilla and cook until golden brown from one side.
4. Place 1/2 C. of fruit onto half the tortilla, followed by the caramel and Brie slices.
5. Fold over the filling and cook until golden brown from both sides.
6. Repeat with the remaining tortillas and filling.
7. Enjoy with a topping of the caramel sauce.

SIMPLE JAM
Quesadillas

Prep Time: 5 mins
Total Time: 20 mins

Servings per Recipe: 2
Calories	424.1
Fat	12.3g
Cholesterol	15.2mg
Sodium	587.9mg
Carbohydrates	70.6g
Protein	7.1g

Ingredients
1 tbsp butter
4 (6 inch) tortillas
4 -6 tbsp jam, any flavor

Directions
1. Place half of the jam onto 2 tortilla shells evenly, leaving about 1/2-inch from the edges.
2. Cover with the remaining tortillas.
3. In a skillet, add half of the butter over medium heat and cook until melted.
4. Place 1 quesadilla and cook until golden brown from both sides.
5. Repeat with the remaining quesadilla.
6. Cut each quesadilla into quarters and enjoy warm.

New England
Spicy Crab Quesadillas

Prep Time: 20 mins
Total Time: 25 mins

Servings per Recipe: 1
Calories	1201.0
Fat	56.9g
Cholesterol	143.1mg
Sodium	2617.2mg
Carbohydrates	122.4g
Protein	47.9g

Ingredients
1/3 C. unsalted butter, melted
1/4 C. vegetable oil
1/2 C. onion, chopped
2 jalapeño peppers, seeded and chopped
1 garlic clove, minced
1 lb. lump crab meat, drained
1/4 C. mayonnaise

1 tbsp cilantro, chopped
1 tsp salt
16 (8 inch) flour tortillas
1/2 C. jalapeño jack cheese, shredded

Directions
1. Set your oven to 375 degrees F before doing anything else
2. In a bowl, add the oil and butter and mix well.
3. In a skillet, add 2 tbsp of the reserved oil mixture over medium heat and cook until heated through.
4. Add the peppers, onion and garlic and stir fry for about 5 minutes.
5. Remove from the heat.
6. Add the crab meat, mayonnaise, cilantro and salt and gently, stir to combine.
7. Coat 1 side of all tortillas with the remaining butter mixture evenly.
8. In the bottom of baking sheets, arrange the tortillas, buttered side down.
9. Place the crab meat mixture onto half of each tortilla, followed by the cheese.
10. Fold each tortilla in half.
11. Cook in the oven for about 4 minutes.
12. Cut each quesadilla into three portions and enjoy warm.

GREEN
Quesadillas

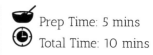

Prep Time: 5 mins
Total Time: 10 mins

Servings per Recipe: 4
Calories	449.6
Fat	22.7g
Cholesterol	50.2mg
Sodium	772.0mg
Carbohydrates	40.5g
Protein	21.0g

Ingredients
4 burrito-size flour tortillas
2 C. grated Monterey jack cheese, packed
1 1/2-2 C. cooked broccoli, chopped

Directions
1. Place a heavy-bottomed skillet over medium heat until heated through.
2. Place 1 tortilla and top with 1/2 C. of the cheese, followed by 1 C. of the broccoli and 1/2 C. of the cheese
3. Cover with another 1 tortilla and cook until golden brown from both sides.
4. Repeat with the remaining tortillas and filling.
5. Cut into wedges and enjoy warm.

Houston

Bacon Ranch Quesadillas

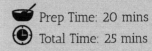 Prep Time: 20 mins

Total Time: 25 mins

Servings per Recipe: 1
Calories	964.1
Fat	81.7g
Cholesterol	116.9mg
Sodium	1801.8mg
Carbohydrates	30.9g
Protein	29.8g

Ingredients

1 flour tortilla
3/4 C. mozzarella cheese, shredded
1 tbsp blue cheese, crumbled
3 slices Roma tomatoes
1/4 avocado, sliced
1/4 C. turkey bacon, cooked crisp, chopped

1 tsp red onion, diced
1 tbsp spinach, julienne
Dressing
1/8 avocado
1/4 C. ranch dressing
3/4 tsp parsley

Directions

1. Place the cheese onto the tortilla evenly.
2. Place the mozzarella cheese over half of the tortilla, followed by the blue cheese, tomatoes, avocado, bacon, onion and spinach.
3. Fold the tortilla in half over the filling.
4. Place a grill pan over medium heat until heated through.
5. Place the quesadilla and cook until golden brown from both sides.
6. Meanwhile, for the dressing: in a food processor, add all the ingredients and pulse until smooth.
7. Cut the quesadilla into 3 portions and enjoy alongside the dressing.

SWEET
Quesadillas for Mommy

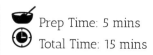

Prep Time: 5 mins
Total Time: 15 mins

Servings per Recipe: 4
Calories	424.2
Fat	12.1g
Cholesterol	22.4mg
Sodium	536.7mg
Carbohydrates	72.0g
Protein	8.4g

Ingredients
cooking spray
1 tbsp butter
2 large flour tortillas
1 (21 oz.) cans apple pie filling
1/2 C. shredded cheddar cheese
1 tbsp sugar
1/4 tsp cinnamon

Directions
1. Set your oven to 375 degrees F before doing anything else and grease a baking sheet.
2. In a microwave-safe bowl, add the butter.
3. With a paper towel, cover the bowl and microwave for about 15 seconds.
4. Place 1 tortilla onto the prepared baking sheet.
5. In the middle of the tortilla, place the apple pie filling, leaving about 1/2-inch around the edges, followed by the cheese.
6. Cover with the second tortilla and top with the butter evenly.
7. In a bowl, add the sugar and cinnamon and mix well.
8. Dust the top of the tortilla with the cinnamon sugar evenly and cook in the oven for about 8-10 minutes.
9. Cut the quesadilla into 4 wedges and enjoy.

Country Spiced
Sweet Potato Quesadillas

🥣 Prep Time: 15 mins
🕐 Total Time: 35 mins

Servings per Recipe: 8
Calories   314.3
Fat   9.7g
Cholesterol   14.8mg
Sodium   561.7mg
Carbohydrates   47.9g
Protein   9.5g

Ingredients

1 1/2 C. onions, minced
2 garlic cloves, minced
1 tbsp olive oil
2 tsp dried oregano
1 1/2 tsp dried basil
1 1/2 tsp dried marjoram
1 1/2 tsp chili powder

1 1/2 tsp ground cumin
4 C. cooked mashed yams
8 whole wheat tortillas
1 C. grated sharp cheddar cheese
salsa
sour cream

Directions

1. Set your oven to 400 degrees F before doing anything else and lightly, grease 1-2 baking sheets.
2. In a skillet, add the oil and cook until heated through.
3. Add the onion and garlic and stir fry for about 4-5 minutes.
4. Add the dried herbs, cumin and chili powder and cumin and stir fry for about 40-50 seconds.
5. Stir in the mashed yams and cook until heated completely.
6. Remove from the heat.
7. Place the yam mixture over half of each tortilla, leaving a 2-inch border at the edge, followed by the cheese.
8. Fold each tortilla over the filling, pressing slightly.
9. In the bottom of the prepared baking sheets, arrange the quesadillas and coat the top of each with the oil.
10. Cook in the oven for about 15-20 minutes.
11. Cut each quesadilla in wedges and enjoy alongside the salsa and sour cream.

PICNIC
Quesadillas

Prep Time: 15 mins
Total Time: 30 mins

Servings per Recipe: 4
Calories	407.9
Fat	25.7g
Cholesterol	77.7mg
Sodium	653.4mg
Carbohydrates	18.9g
Protein	24.4g

Ingredients
4 flour tortillas
3/4 C. shredded cheddar cheese
1 (8 oz.) sirloin steaks, grilled, sliced
1 jalapeño, minced
3/4 C. salsa, drained of excess liquid
1 tbsp vegetable oil

Directions
1. Place about 1/4 C. of the cheese onto each of 2 tortillas evenly, followed by the steak, jalapeño, 1/4 C. of the salsa and remaining cheese.
2. Cover each with the remaining tortillas and press to seal.
3. In a skillet add 1 1/2 tsp of the oil over medium heat and cook until heated through.
4. Place quesadillas, 1 at a time and cook for about 4-6 minutes, flipping once half way through.
5. Enjoy warm.

Weekend
Ground Beef Quesadillas

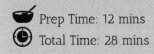 Prep Time: 12 mins
Total Time: 28 mins

Servings per Recipe: 2
Calories   255.6
Fat   17.5g
Cholesterol   42.5mg
Sodium   1053.3mg
Carbohydrates   9.7g
Protein   18.1g

Ingredients
1/3 C. cooked extra lean ground beef
3 tbsp taco sauce
4 large burrito-size whole wheat tortillas
4 oz. blue cheese, crumbled
10 oz. frozen chopped spinach, thawed
and squeezed dry
1/2 tsp red pepper flakes

Directions
1. In a bowl, add the taco sauce and beef and mix well.
2. Arrange 2 tortillas onto a platter and top each with the beef mixture, followed by the cheese, spinach and red pepper flakes.
3. Cover each with remaining tortilla.
4. Place a nonstick skillet over medium-high heat until heated through.
5. Place 1 quesadilla and cook until golden brown from both sides.
6. Transfer the quesadilla onto a plate.
7. Repeat with the remaining quesadilla.
8. Cut each quesadilla into desired sized wedges and enjoy.

COOKOUT
Chicken Quesadillas

Prep Time: 5 mins
Total Time: 10 mins

Servings per Recipe: 8
Calories   509.9
Fat   18.2g
Cholesterol   46.3mg
Sodium   999.4mg
Carbohydrates   60.6g
Protein   24.0g

Ingredients

2 C. cooked chicken, chopped
1/2 C. barbecue sauce
1 tbsp onion, minced
8 large flour tortillas
6 - 8 oz. Monterey Jack cheese, grated

Directions

1. In a pot, add the chicken, onion and barbecue sauce and cook until just heated.
2. Meanwhile, with a 3-inch cookie cutters, cut each tortilla into rounds.
3. Place the cheese onto half of tortilla pieces evenly, followed by the chicken mixture and a little more cheese.
4. Cover with the remaining tortilla pieces.
5. Place a nonstick skillet over medium heat until heated through.
6. Place the mini quesadillas in batches and cook for about 4 minutes, flipping once half way through.
7. Enjoy warm.

5-Ingredient
Mushroom Quesadillas

🥣 Prep Time: 5 mins
🕐 Total Time: 20 mins

Servings per Recipe: 2
Calories	217.7
Fat	4.9g
Cholesterol	0.0mg
Sodium	386.6mg
Carbohydrates	36.6g
Protein	7.5g

Ingredients
1/2 large onion, chopped
5 oz. sliced mushrooms
cheddar cheese, shredded
4 flour tortillas
butter

Directions
1. Place a greased skillet over medium heat until heated through.
2. Add the onion and stir fry for about 4-5 minutes.
3. Add the mushrooms and cook for about 6 minutes.
4. Transfer the mushroom mixture into a bowl.
5. Place the butter onto 1 side of each tortilla.
6. Place the mushroom mixture onto unbuttered side of 2 tortillas evenly, followed by the cheddar cheese.
7. Cover with the remaining tortillas, buttered side up.
8. Place a nonstick skillet over medium-low heat.
9. Place the quesadillas, 1 at a time and cook for until golden brown from both sides.
10. Cut each quesadilla in quarters and enjoy.

CANCUN
Havarti Quesadillas

Prep Time: 15 mins
Total Time: 23 mins

Servings per Recipe: 4
Calories   60.4
Fat   0.2g
Cholesterol   0.0mg
Sodium   2.4mg
Carbohydrates   11.0g
Protein   4.0g

Ingredients
8 small whole wheat tortillas
1 C. black beans, rinsed and drained
1/2 C. red bell pepper, chopped
3 green onions, chopped
2 tbsp cilantro, chopped
2 C. Havarti cheese, diced

Directions
1. Place the black beans onto 4 tortillas, followed by the bell pepper, green onions,
2. cilantro and cheese.
3. Cover with the remaining tortillas.
4. Place a nonstick skillet over medium heat until heated through.
5. Add the tortilla sandwiches, 1 at a time and cook for about 8 minutes, flipping once half way through.
6. Enjoy warm.

Maria's
Spinach Quesadillas

Prep Time: 15 mins
Total Time: 20 mins

Servings per Recipe: 4
Calories	924.5
Fat	56.0g
Cholesterol	102.6mg
Sodium	1850.1mg
Carbohydrates	71.9g
Protein	33.8g

Ingredients
Relish
1/2 red onion, sliced
3/4 C. oil-cured black olive, chopped
2 tbsp grated lemon zest
2 tbsp apple cider vinegar
1/4 C. extra virgin olive oil
salt
ground black pepper
Quesadillas

12 (6 inch) flour tortillas
2 C. white cheddar cheese, grated
1 C. crumbled feta
6 oz. Baby Spinach
salt
ground black pepper
olive oil

Directions
1. For the relish: in a bowl, add all the ingredients and mix until well combined.
2. Cover the bowl and place in the fridge before using.
3. Set your grill for medium heat and lightly, grease the grill grate.
4. Place the cheeses onto 8 tortillas evenly, followed by the spinach and sprinkle with the salt and pepper.
5. Arrange 4 filled tortillas onto other 2 filled tortillas, filling side up.
6. Cover with the remaining plain tortillas.
7. Coat the top of each quesadilla with the oil evenly.
8. Arrange the quesadillas onto the grill, oiled side down and cook for about 2 minutes.
9. Carefully, flip each quesadilla and cook, covered for about 1-2 minutes.
10. Cut each quesadilla into quarters and enjoy with a topping of the relish.

ONTARIO TOPPED
Chicken Quesadillas

Prep Time: 15 mins
Total Time: 30 mins

Servings per Recipe: 5	
Calories	135.0
Fat	13.4g
Cholesterol	6.1mg
Sodium	20.1mg
Carbohydrates	3.0g
Protein	2.2g

Ingredients

4 tbsp vegetable oil
4 garlic cloves, minced
2 bunches red Swiss chard, cleaned & chopped
12 oz. mushrooms
1/2 C. chicken
1 tbsp butter
1 tsp apple cider vinegar
cheddar cheese, grated

about 10 corn tortilla
organic sour cream
organic cilantro
organic guacamole

Directions

1. In a pot, add the oil over medium-high heat and cook until heated through.
2. Add the garlic and stir fry for about 30 seconds.
3. Add the mushrooms and stir fry for about 5-6 minutes.
4. Add the chard and cook until wilted slightly.
5. Add the broth and cook, covered until the chard is cooked through.
6. Stir in the vinegar and butter and cook, uncovered until all the moisture is absorbed.
7. Divide half of the cheese onto 5 tortillas evenly, followed by the veggie mixture and remaining cheese.
8. Cover with the remaining tortillas.
9. In a nonstick skillet, add a little of the butter and cook until melted.
10. Place 1 quesadilla at a time and cook until golden brown from both sides.
11. Enjoy with a garnishing of the guacamole, sour cream and cilantro.

Classical
Mediterranean Quesadillas

Prep Time: 5 mins
Total Time: 25 mins

Servings per Recipe: 4

Calories	312.2
Fat	13.0g
Cholesterol	26.4mg
Sodium	857.3mg
Carbohydrates	35.3g
Protein	13.8g

Ingredients

1 tsp olive oil
cooking spray
1/3 C. chopped onion
1/2 tsp minced garlic
1 1/4 C. shredded zucchini
1/4 tsp dried oregano
1/8 tsp salt
1/8 tsp black pepper
4 (8 inch) fat-free flour tortillas

1/2 C. shredded part-skim mozzarella cheese, divided
1/2 C. diced tomato, divided
1/4 C. chopped pitted kalamata olive, divided
1/4 C. crumbled feta cheese, divided

Directions

1. In a nonstick skillet, add the oil over medium-high heat until heated through.
2. Add the garlic and onion and stir fry for about 2 minutes.
3. Add the zucchini and stir fry for about 3 minutes.
4. Remove from the heat and stir in the oregano, salt and pepper.
5. Place mozzarella onto 2 tortillas evenly, followed by the zucchini mixture, tomato, olives and feta.
6. Cover with remaining tortillas.
7. Grease another skillet with the cooking spray and place over medium heat until heated through.
8. Place 1 quesadilla and cook for about 2 1/2 minutes per side.
9. Repeat with the remaining quesadilla.
10. Cut each quesadilla in half and enjoy warm.

HOT PEAR
Quesadillas

🥣 Prep Time: 20 mins
🕐 Total Time: 40 mins

Servings per Recipe: 10
Calories   180.4
Fat   12.5g
Cholesterol   34.0mg
Sodium   241.8mg
Carbohydrates   10.1g
Protein   7.6g

Ingredients

12 oz. chilled Brie cheese, cut into strips
2 pears, ripe and sliced
1/2 red onion, sliced
2 jalapeño peppers, seeded and sliced
6 inches flour tortillas
2 tbsp olive oil

Directions

1. Place the Brie cheese onto the bottom half of each tortilla evenly, followed by the pear and jalapeño slices.

2. Fold each tortilla in half over the filling.

3. In a skillet add 1 tsp of the oil and cook until heated through.

4. Add 1 quesadilla and cook until golden brown from all sides.

5. Repeat with the remaining quesadillas.

6. Enjoy warm.

Garden Tuna
Quesadillas

Prep Time: 10 mins
Total Time: 22 mins

Servings per Recipe: 4

Calories	257.6
Fat	18.2g
Cholesterol	53.5mg
Sodium	247.9mg
Carbohydrates	2.3g
Protein	20.9g

Ingredients

4 pesto garlic tortillas
1 tbsp olive oil
1/4 C. roasted red pepper pesto
2 (85 g) tuna, drained
2 C. zucchini, grated
6 slices Monterey Jack pepper cheese
salt and pepper

Directions

1. Coat each side of all tortillas with a thin layer of the oil.
2. Place the pesto onto 2 tortillas evenly, followed by the tuna, zucchini and cheese slices.
3. Sprinkle with the salt and pepper and cover with the remaining 2 tortillas, oiled side up.
4. In a skillet, place 1 quesadilla over medium heat, oiled side down and cook for about 2-3 minutes per side.
5. Repeat with the remaining quesadilla.
6. Cut each quesadilla into 6 wedges and enjoy.

SWEET
Carolina Apple Quesadillas

Prep Time: 30 mins
Total Time: 42 mins

Servings per Recipe: 6
Calories	679.2
Fat	38.8g
Cholesterol	77.4mg
Sodium	750.6mg
Carbohydrates	76.9g
Protein	10.1g

Ingredients
2 granny smith apples, sliced
1/2 C. dried sweetened cranberries
1 tsp cinnamon sugar
1 tsp lemon juice
7 tbsp butter, divided
6 10-inch flour tortillas
1 (8 oz.) packages cream cheese, softened
1/4 C. powdered sugar
1/2 C. caramel sauce

1/2 C. chopped pecans, toasted

Directions
1. In a bowl, add the apples, cranberries, cinnamon sugar and lemon juice and toss to coat well.
2. In a nonstick skillet, a 1 tbsp of the butter over medium heat and cook until melted.
3. Add the apple mixture and stir fry for about 4-5 minutes.
4. With a slotted spoon, place the apple mixture into a bowl.
5. In a bowl, add the powdered sugar and cream cheese and beat until smooth.
6. Place 1 tbsp of the butter onto 1 side of all tortillas evenly.
7. Place the cream cheese mixture onto another side of all tortillas evenly, followed by the apple mixture.
8. Carefully, fold each tortilla in half over the filling.
9. Place a skillet over medium heat until heated through.
10. Place the quesadillas and cook for about 4 minutes, flipping once half way through.
11. Transfer the quesadillas onto a platter and drizzle with the caramel sauce.
12. Enjoy with a topping of the pecans.

Parmesan
Pepper Quesadillas

Prep Time: 5 mins
Total Time: 10 mins

Servings per Recipe: 4
Calories	386.3
Fat	20.5g
Cholesterol	21.7mg
Sodium	668.7mg
Carbohydrates	38.2g
Protein	11.9g

Ingredients

1 tbsp green pepper, chopped
1/4 C. Parmesan cheese
1/2 C. grated cheddar cheese
1/4 C. chopped green onion
1 1/2 tbsp mayonnaise
4 tortillas
2 tbsp oil

Directions

1. Set your barbecue grill for medium heat and lightly, grease the grill grate.
2. In a bowl, add the Parmesan cheese, cheddar cheese, mayonnaise, green pepper and green onion and mix until well combined.
3. Place the cheese mixture onto 2 tortillas evenly.
4. Cover with the remaining 2 tortillas.
5. Cot the both sides of each quesadilla with the oil evenly.
6. Cook the quesadillas onto the grill for about 5 minutes.
7. Enjoy warm.

VEGETARIAN
Black Bean Quesadillas

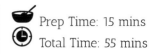

Prep Time: 15 mins

Total Time: 55 mins

Servings per Recipe: 1
Calories	349.3
Fat	13.3g
Cholesterol	25.1mg
Sodium	514.9mg
Carbohydrates	43.6g
Protein	14.8g

Ingredients
8 (8 inch) flour tortillas
1 C. frozen corn, thawed
1 C. black beans, cooked
2/3 red onion, thin slivers
2 C. Monterey Jack cheese, grated
1 tsp chili powder

Directions
1. Place the corn onto 4 tortillas evenly, leaving about 1/2-inch edges, followed by the beans, onion, cheese and chili powder.
2. Cover with the remaining tortillas and gently, press down.
3. Place a lightly greased skillet over medium heat until heated through.
4. Add quesadillas, 1 at a time and cook for about 8-10 minutes, flipping once half way through.
5. Cut each quesadilla into 4 wedges and enjoy.

Arizona
Deli Quesadillas

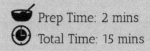 Prep Time: 2 mins
Total Time: 15 mins

Servings per Recipe: 4
Calories   218.4
Fat   5.4g
Cholesterol   0.0mg
Sodium   445.2mg
Carbohydrates   35.9g
Protein   5.8g

Ingredients
4 burrito-size flour tortillas
6 -8 oz. Pepper Jack Cheese, shredded
8 oz. Deli-Thin Slices Turkey
1/2 C. pickled jalapeño pepper, drained

Directions
1. Set your grill for low heat and lightly, grease the grill grate.
2. Arrange the tortillas onto the grill grate.
3. Divide half of the cheese onto one side of each tortilla evenly, followed by the turkey , jalapeños and remaining cheese.
4. carefully, fold each tortillas in half over the filling.
5. Cook onto the grill for about 3-4 minutes, flipping once half way through.
6. Enjoy hot.

REAL
Mexicana Quesadillas

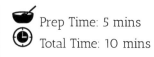 Prep Time: 5 mins
Total Time: 10 mins

Servings per Recipe: 1
Calories	604.3
Fat	27.2g
Cholesterol	48.0mg
Sodium	1450.8mg
Carbohydrates	64.7g
Protein	24.2g

Ingredients
1 large flour tortilla
75 g grated cheese
8 -12 slices of pickled green jalapeño
peppers
cooking spray

Directions
1. Grease a skillet with the cooking spray and place over medium heat until heated through.
2. Place the tortilla and cook until golden brown from 1 side.
3. Transfer the tortilla onto a plate, browned side down.
4. Place the cheese onto the bottom half of the tortilla, followed by the jalapeños.
5. Carefully, fold each tortilla in half over the filling.
6. Coat the both sides of each quesadilla with the cooking spray.
7. Place the quesadillas into the same skillet and cook until golden brown from both sides.
8. Cut each quesadilla into 2-4 slices and enjoy.

Hot Mediterranean
Mozzarella Quesadillas

Prep Time: 10 mins
Total Time: 20 mins

Servings per Recipe: 12
Calories	237.1
Fat	11.2g
Cholesterol	20.5mg
Sodium	550.6mg
Carbohydrates	25.0g
Protein	8.8g

Ingredients

2 pieces chili peppers, chopped
200 g mozzarella cheese, granted
100 g feta cheese
16 green olives, without stones
6 tsp coriander leaves, chopped
8 tortillas
4 tsp olive oil
2 tsp paprika

Directions

1. Set your oven to 425 degrees F before doing anything else.
2. In a blender, add the olives, chilies, coriander, feta and mozzarella cheese and pulse until smooth and creamy.
3. In a bowl, add the oil and paprika and mix well.
4. Arrange 4 tortillas onto a baking sheet and top with the cheese mixture evenly.
5. Cover with the remaining 4 tortillas and coat each with the paprika oil.
6. With a piece of the foil, cover the baking sheet and cook in the oven for about 5 minutes.
7. Cut each quesadilla into 8 wedges and enjoy.

BREAKFAST
Quesadillas

Prep Time: 10 mins
Total Time: 20 mins

Servings per Recipe: 2
Calories	231.1
Fat	8.1g
Cholesterol	27.3mg
Sodium	917.2mg
Carbohydrates	22.0g
Protein	17.9g

Ingredients
1 C. sliced mushrooms
2 tbsp chopped onions
1/2 C. egg substitute
2 tbsp chopped tomatoes
2 flour tortillas, 10-inch
4 (1/2 oz.) turkey slices
1/4 C. shredded mozzarella cheese
1/4 C. shredded reduced-fat cheddar
cheese

3 tbsp salsa

Directions
1. Place a greased nonstick skillet over medium heat until heated through.
2. Add the onion and mushrooms and stir fry for about 4-5 minutes.
3. Add the tomato and egg substitute and cook until egg mixture becomes set.
4. Place a nonstick skillet over medium heat until heated through.
5. Place 1 tortilla and top with turkey , followed by the egg mixture and cheeses.
6. Cover with the remaining tortillas.
7. Cook until golden brown from both sides.
8. Cut into 4 wedges and enjoy with a topping of the salsa.

Dorm Room
Fruit Quesadillas

Prep Time: 10 mins
Total Time: 25 mins

Servings per Recipe: 4
Calories	661.1
Fat	38.7g
Cholesterol	104.7mg
Sodium	1267.6mg
Carbohydrates	51.6g
Protein	28.1g

Ingredients
6 whole wheat tortillas
12 oz. cheddar cheese, shredded
2 apples, washed and sliced
2 tbsp butter
1 - 2 tbsp butter

Directions
1. Place 3 tbsp of the cheese over one half of each tortilla, followed by the apple slices and 2 tbsp of the cheese.
2. Carefully, fold each tortilla in half over the filling.
3. In a skillet, add the butter over medium - high heat and cook until melted.
4. Place the quesadillas, 1 at a time and cook until golden brown from both sides.
5. Enjoy warm.

WEEKNIGHT
Leftover Quesadillas

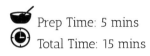 Prep Time: 5 mins

Total Time: 15 mins

Servings per Recipe: 1

Calories	526.0
Fat	26.4g
Cholesterol	69.3mg
Sodium	1676.7mg
Carbohydrates	50.3g
Protein	22.1g

Ingredients

2 (6 inch) tortillas, warmed
2 tbsp salsa, divided
2/3 C. chopped leftover meatloaf, divided
1/2 C. shredded Mexican cheese, divided
oil

Directions

1. Place about the salsa onto half of each tortilla evenly, followed by the meatloaf and cheese.
2. Fold each tortilla in half over the filling.
3. In a nonstick skillet, add the oil over medium-high heat and cook until heated through.
4. Place the quesadillas, 1 at a time and cook for about 5 minutes per side.
5. Cut each quesadillas in half and enjoy.

Monterey Chili
Quesadillas with Handmade Tortillas

Prep Time: 30 mins
Total Time: 40 mins

Servings per Recipe: 6
Calories	314.8
Fat	15.2g
Cholesterol	33.5mg
Sodium	497.9mg
Carbohydrates	32.7g
Protein	13.3g

Ingredients

Tortillas
2 C. masa harina
1 1/4 C. plus 2 tbsp warm water
1/4 tsp salt
Insides
1 tbsp canola oil
1 white onion, sliced
2 garlic cloves, chopped
1/2 tsp dried oregano

2 poblano chilies, roasted, peeled, seeded, then cut lengthwise into strips
1/2 tsp sea salt
2 C. Monterey Jack cheese, shredded
canola oil
guacamole, and salsa

Directions

1. For the tortillas: in a bowl, add the warm water and masa harina and with your hands. Mix until a smooth and pliable dough is formed.
2. With a slightly damp kitchen towel, cover the bowl and keep aside for about 5-10 minutes.
3. Add the salt and with your hands, knead for about 1 minute.
4. Make 12 equal sized balls from the dough.
5. With a damp kitchen towel, cover the balls and keep aside until using.
6. For the filling: in a skillet, add the oil over medium heat and cook until heated through.
7. Add the onion and stir fry for about 6 minutes.
8. Stir in the oregano and garlic and cook for about 40 seconds.
9. Stir in the chilies and salt and cook until heated completely, tossing frequently.
10. Arrange a dough ball between 2 plastic sheets and with a rolling pin, roll into a circular shape.
11. Remove the top plastic sheet and top the tortilla with some cheese, leaving the edges,

followed by the chile strips and onion slices.

12. Carefully, fold the uncovered side of the tortilla over the filling and with your fingers, press the edges together.

13. Place onto a baking sheet and cover with a damp towel.

14. Repeat with the remaining dough balls and filling.

15. In a heavy bottomed skillet, add about 1-inch of the oil over medium-high heat until heated through.

16. Place the quesadillas, 1 at a time and fry for about 1-2 minutes.

17. With a slotted spoon, transfer the fried quesadillas onto a paper towel-lined plate to drain.

18. Enjoy hot.

Salsa Swiss
Quesadillas

Prep Time: 5 mins
Total Time: 6 mins

Servings per Recipe: 1
Calories	593.8
Fat	23.6g
Cholesterol	41.7mg
Sodium	987.0mg
Carbohydrates	73.7g
Protein	20.2g

Ingredients
1 slice Swiss cheese
1 tbsp cream cheese
2 tortillas
salsa

Directions
1. Place the cream cheese onto to 1 tortilla, followed by the cream cheese.
2. Cover with the remaining tortilla.
3. Cook in the toaster oven until desired level of crunchiness.
4. Cut the quesadilla into triangles and enjoy alongside the salsa.

BACON LETTUCE and Tomato Quesadillas

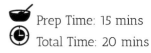 Prep Time: 15 mins

Total Time: 20 mins

Servings per Recipe: 4
Calories	741.1
Fat	41.6g
Cholesterol	56.9mg
Sodium	1329.7mg
Carbohydrates	64.5g
Protein	26.7g

Ingredients
4 large flour tortillas
8 oz. soft goat cheese
1 tsp cumin
1 lb. tomatoes, stemmed & sliced
2 tsp balsamic vinegar
8 pieces turkey bacon, cooked crisp and drained then cut into pieces
2 C. Baby Spinach
olive oil

Directions
1. Set your grill for medium-low heat and lightly, grease the grill grate.
2. In a bowl, add the cumin and cheese and mix until well combined.
3. Place the cheese mixture onto each tortilla evenly, followed by the tomatoes, vinegar, bacon pieces and spinach.
4. Fold each tortilla in half over the filling and press down together.
5. Place the quesadillas and cook for about 4 minutes, flipping once half way through, pressing with a spatula.
6. Cut each quesadilla into 3 wedges and enjoy.

Full Quesadilla Dinner (Chicken and Beans)

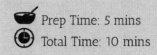 Prep Time: 5 mins
Total Time: 10 mins

Servings per Recipe: 1

Calories	885.9
Fat	53.0g
Cholesterol	144.1mg
Sodium	1349.9mg
Carbohydrates	68.8g
Protein	33.8g

Ingredients

1 large flour tortilla
1 oz. chopped cooked chicken
1 oz. refried beans
1 oz. sliced onion
1 oz. sliced bell pepper
1 oz. sliced raw mushrooms
2 tbsp butter
2 oz. shredded cheddar cheese

Directions

1. In a cast iron skillet, add 1 tbsp of the butter and cook until melted.
2. Add the mushrooms, peppers and onions and cook for about 6 - 8 minutes.
3. Place the beans onto one half of the tortilla, followed by the chicken, cheese and mushroom mixture.
4. Fold the tortilla in half over the filling.
5. In another skillet, add the remaining butter and cook until melted.
6. Place the quesadilla and cook for about 2 minutes, flipping once half way through.
7. Cut the quesadilla into 4 wedges and enjoy.

EASY
Quesadilla Souvlaki

Prep Time: 5 mins
Total Time: 15 mins

Servings per Recipe: 2
Calories   253.9
Fat   15.7g
Cholesterol   92.0mg
Sodium   625.8mg
Carbohydrates   2.1g
Protein   24.8g

Ingredients
1 cooked boneless skinless chicken breast
1/2 C. mozzarella cheese
1/2 C. feta cheese
1/4 C. sautéed onion
2 (10 inch) whole wheat tortillas

Directions
1. Place a lightly greased skillet over medium-high heat until heated through.
2. Place 1 tortilla and cook until golden brown.
3. Transfer the tortilla onto a plate.
4. Grease the skillet again.
5. Place the remaining tortilla and top with the cheeses, followed by the chicken.
6. Cover with the toasted tortilla, browned side upward and cook until cheese melts completely.
7. Cut the quesadilla into wedges and enjoy.

Hot
Shrimp Quesadillas

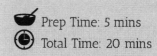 Prep Time: 5 mins

Total Time: 20 mins

Servings per Recipe: 6

Calories	362.0
Fat	18.9g
Cholesterol	36.5mg
Sodium	604.9mg
Carbohydrates	33.1g
Protein	14.8g

Ingredients

1 (4 oz.) cans chopped green chilies, drained
2 C. cooked shrimp, chopped
1 C. chopped spinach
1 tbsp olive oil
1 C. shredded Monterey Jack pepper cheese
1 C. shredded cheddar cheese
1 tbsp chopped cilantro

12 flour tortillas
nonstick cooking spray

Directions

1. In a skillet, add the oil and cook until heated through.
2. Add the spinach and cook until wilted.
3. Remove from the heat.
4. In a bowl, add the shrimp, spinach, chilies, cilantro, cheddar and pepper jack cheese and mix well.
5. Coat one side of all tortillas with the cooking spray.
6. Place a skillet over medium heat until heated through.
7. Place 1 tortilla, greased side down and top with 1/6 of the shrimp mixture.
8. Cover with another 1 tortilla, greased side up and cook for about 4 minutes, flipping once half way through.
9. Repeat with the remaining tortillas and shrimp mixture.
10. Cut each quesadilla in 4 wedges and enjoy.

PICO DE GALLO
Quesadillas

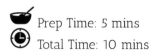

Prep Time: 5 mins
Total Time: 10 mins

Servings per Recipe: 1
Calories	54.4
Fat	0.8g
Cholesterol	0.4mg
Sodium	11.3mg
Carbohydrates	10.7g
Protein	1.4g

Ingredients
2 (6 inch) corn tortillas
4 slices manchego cheese
1/2 tsp sour cream
1 tsp pico de gallo
cooking spray

Directions
1. Place 2 manchego cheese slices onto each tortilla.
2. Fold each tortilla in half over the cheese.
3. Grease a skillet with the cooking spray and place over heat until heated through.
4. Place the quesadillas, 1 at a time and cook for about 4-6 minutes, flipping once half way through.
5. Enjoy hot with a topping of the sour cream and Pico de Gallo.

My First
Quesadilla (Macaroni and Cheese)

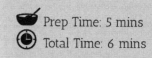 Prep Time: 5 mins

Total Time: 6 mins

Servings per Recipe: 2
Calories   218.4
Fat   5.4g
Cholesterol   0.0mg
Sodium   445.2mg
Carbohydrates   35.9g
Protein   5.8g

Ingredients
2 tortillas
1/2 C. prepared macaroni and cheese
1 slice cheese

Directions
1. In a microwave-safe plate, place 1 tortilla and top with the Mac and Cheese, followed by the cheese.
2. Cover with the remaining tortilla and microwave for about 1 3/4 minutes.
3. Cut the quesadilla into 4 wedges and enjoy.

TROPICAL
Texas Quesadillas

Prep Time: 8 mins
Total Time: 18 mins

Servings per Recipe: 2
Calories	1294.9
Fat	87.0g
Cholesterol	126.0mg
Sodium	4167.3mg
Carbohydrates	89.0g
Protein	40.9g

Ingredients
1 C. chopped pineapple
4 tortillas, of any brand
2 C. chopped chicken breasts
2 C. shredded sharp cheddar cheese
3 tbsp Hidden Valley® Original Ranch®
Dressing
2 tsp onion powder
2 tsp pepper
2 tsp salt

1/4 C. olive oil

Directions
1. For the dressing: in a skillet, add the oil, onion powder, salt and pepper and cook until heated.
2. Add the chicken and cook for about 6-8 minutes.
3. Remove from the heat.
4. Place the cheddar onto 2 tortillas evenly, followed by the ranch dressing, pineapples and chicken.
5. Cover with the remaining tortillas.
6. In the same skillet, place the quesadillas, 1 at a time and cook until golden brown from both sides.
7. Cut into 4 wedges and enjoy.

Monterey
Beef Quesadillas

Prep Time: 10 mins
Total Time: 30 mins

Servings per Recipe: 4
Calories   1495.7
Fat   143.2g
Cholesterol   231.7mg
Sodium   698.9mg
Carbohydrates   17.5g
Protein   32.6g

Ingredients
1 1/2 lb. beef, strips
2 tbsp creole seasoning
1 tsp onion powder
1 tsp garlic powder
1/2 tsp black pepper
8 oz. of shredded Monterey Jack pepper cheese
4 tbsp of crumbled feta cheese
4 flour tortillas

nonstick cooking spray
sour cream

Directions
1. Heat a pan and cook the beef, creole seasoning, garlic powder, onion powder and black pepper for about 9-10 minutes.
2. Drain the grease from the pan.
3. Place the pepper Jack cheese onto one half of all tortillas evenly, followed by the feta and beef mixture.
4. Fold each tortilla in half over the filling.
5. Place a greased nonstick skillet over medium-high heat and cook the quesadillas for about 4-6 minutes, flinging once half way through.
6. Cut each quesadilla in half and enjoy alongside the sour cream.

COUNTRY
Cranberry Quesadillas

Prep Time: 5 mins
Total Time: 15 mins

Servings per Recipe: 12
Calories	142.8
Fat	7.9g
Cholesterol	18.9mg
Sodium	246.9mg
Carbohydrates	12.1g
Protein	5.7g

Ingredients
1 tbsp extra virgin olive oil
1 C. sliced yellow onion
8 flour tortillas
1/2 lb. soft Brie cheese
1/2 C. dried cranberries
ground black pepper
cilantro leaf

Directions
1. Set your oven to 425 degrees F before doing anything else.
2. In a skillet, add the oil over medium heat and cook until heated through.
3. Add the onion and cook for about 4 minutes, mixing often.
4. Transfer the onions into a bowl and keep aside to cool.
5. In the bottom of a baking sheet, place 4 tortillas and top each with the Brie cheese, followed by the cooked onions, cranberries and black pepper.
6. Cover with the remaining tortillas.
7. Cook in the oven for about 8 minutes.
8. Cut each quesadilla into 6 equal sized wedges and enjoy with a garnishing of the cilantro leaves.

Hot
Cauliflower Quesadillas

Prep Time: 5 mins
Total Time: 10 mins

Servings per Recipe: 1
Calories   2319.0
Fat   157.1g
Cholesterol   122.6mg
Sodium   3279.2mg
Carbohydrates   204.0g
Protein   44.2g

Ingredients

2 tbsp olive oil
2 C. cauliflower florets, sliced
4 tbsp hot sauce
1/2 tsp chili powder
1/2 tsp garlic powder
1/2 tsp snipped chives
10 inches spinach tortillas
3 tbsp cream cheese
1/2 C. shredded mozzarella cheese

1 tbsp butter
1 avocado, mashed
10 tortilla chips, crushed

Directions

1. In a bowl, add the cauliflower, 3 tbsp of the hot sauce, garlic powder and chili powder and mix well.
2. In a skillet, add the oil and cook until heated through.
3. Add the cauliflower and cook for about 3 minutes, mixing often.
4. Transfer the cauliflower into a bowl.
5. Add the chives and remaining 1 tbsp of the hot sauce and gently, toss to coat.
6. Place the cream cheese onto the tortilla in a thin layer.
7. Place the cauliflower mixture onto half of the tortilla, followed by the mozzarella.
8. Fold tortilla in half over the filling.
9. In a nonstick skillet, add the butter and cook until melted.
10. Place the quesadilla and cook until golden brown from both sides.
11. Cut the quesadilla into 3 wedges and enjoy with a topping of the avocado, Takis and chives.

NOVEMBER
Yam Quesadillas

Prep Time: 15 mins
Total Time: 1 hr 10 mins

Servings per Recipe: 4

Calories	505.7
Fat	13.2g
Cholesterol	0.0mg
Sodium	764.4mg
Carbohydrates	82.8g
Protein	14.6g

Ingredients
2 large sweet potatoes, peeled and sliced
into chunks
4 large flour tortillas
1 tsp smoked paprika
1 tsp cumin
1/2 tsp ground coriander
1/4 tsp cayenne pepper
2/3 C. black beans, rinsed
1/2 lime. juiced

1/4 tsp salt and black pepper
1/4 C. raw cashews
1/4 C. nutritional yeast with 1 tsp water

Directions
1. Set your oven to 425 degrees F before doing anything else.
2. In a baking dish, place the sweet potato, coriander, cumin, cayenne pepper, paprika, salt and pepper and mix well.
3. Cook in the oven for about 30 - 40 minutes.
4. Meanwhile, for the nutritional yeast cheese: in a blender, add cashews, nutritional yeast and water and pulse until smooth.
5. Remove from the oven and keep aside to cool slightly.
6. With a potato masher, mash the sweet potatoes roughly.
7. Place the mashed sweet potato onto 2 tortillas evenly, followed by the black beans, nutritional yeast cheese, a little lime juice and seasoning.
8. Cover with the remaining tortillas.
9. Place a skillet over medium heat until heated through.
10. Cook for about 6 - 8 minutes per side.
11. Enjoy warm.

Greek
Quesadillas

Prep Time: 10 mins
Total Time: 25 mins

Servings per Recipe: 4
Calories	180.4
Fat	9.5g
Cholesterol	0.0mg
Sodium	224.3mg
Carbohydrates	20.2g
Protein	4.1g

Ingredients
2 tbsp extra virgin olive oil, divided
1/2 lb. fresh asparagus, cut into pieces
salt and pepper
2 (10 inch) flour tortillas
4 oz. herbed goat cheese
1/4 C. chopped cilantro
cilantro stem

Directions
1. In a skillet, add 1 tbsp of the oil over medium-low heat and cook until heated through.
2. Add the asparagus and cook until tender, mixing often.
3. Stir in the salt and pepper and remove from the heat.
4. Place the goat cheese onto both tortillas, followed by the asparagus and cilantro.
5. Fold each tortilla in half over the filling.
6. Coat the both sides of each quesadilla with the remaining oil.
7. Place a skillet over medium-low heat and cook until heated through.
8. Add the quesadillas, 1 at a time and cook for about 6 minutes, flipping once half way through.
9. Cut each quesadilla into half and enjoy with a garnishing of the cilantro sprigs.

MUSHROOM
Quesadillas with Homemade Blue Tortillas

Prep Time: 5 mins
Total Time: 45 mins

Servings per Recipe: 6
Calories	16.8
Fat	0.1g
Cholesterol	0.0mg
Sodium	3.2mg
Carbohydrates	3.1g
Protein	1.4g

Ingredients
Mushroom
2 tbsp olive oil
1 onion, sliced
8 oz. porcini mushrooms, trimmed and sliced
1 jalapeño chili, seeded and minced
salt & ground black pepper
3 sprigs of cilantro
Tortillas

1 C. blue cornmeal
1 C. masa harina
1/2 tsp salt
about 1 C. warm water
1 C. queso fresco
salsa

Directions
1. In a heavy-bottomed skillet, add the oil over medium heat and cook until heated through.
2. Add the onions and stir fry for about 4 minutes.
3. Add the chilies and mushrooms and cook for about 6 minutes.
4. Stir in the cilantro, salt and pepper and remove from the heat.
5. For the tortillas: in a bowl, add the masa harina, cornmeal, salt and warm water and with a wooden spoon, mix until a dough forms.
6. With a plastic wrap, cover the bowl tightly and keep aside for about 2 minutes.
7. Make 12 balls from the dough.
8. Place a ball between 2 plastic sheets and with the palm of your hand, flatten slightly.
9. Now, with a rolling pin, roll the ball into a 6-inch circle.
10. Repeat with the remaining dough balls.
11. Place a skillet over high heat.
12. Place the tortillas, 1 at a time and cook for about 1 minute, flipping once half way through.
13. Place the cheese onto 6 tortillas, followed by the mushroom mixture.
14. Cover with the remaining tortillas.
15. Place the quesadillas, 1 at a time over medium-high heat and cook until golden brown from both sides.
16. Cut each quesadilla into wedges and enjoy alongside the salsa.

Light Lunch
Quesadillas (Tomatoes and Capers)

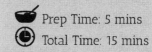 Prep Time: 5 mins

Total Time: 15 mins

Servings per Recipe: 1
Calories	341.5
Fat	15.6g
Cholesterol	31.9mg
Sodium	796.1mg
Carbohydrates	43.3g
Protein	8.5g

Ingredients
1 tortilla
2 - 3 tbsp cream cheese
1/2 Roma tomato, sliced
2 - 3 tbsp red onions, sliced
1 tbsp capers
1/2 lemon, juiced

Directions
1. Place the cream cheese onto one half of the tortilla, followed by the tomato, onions, capers and
2. lemon juice.
3. Carefully, fold the tortilla in half over the filling.
4. Place a greased skillet over medium-high heat until heated through.
5. Place the quesadilla and cook for about 1 1/2-2 minutes per side.
6. Cut the quesadilla into wedges and enjoy.

BROOKLYN
Cheesecake Quesadillas

Prep Time: 3 mins
Total Time: 6 mins

Servings per Recipe: 4
Calories   336.6
Fat   21.8g
Cholesterol   62.4mg
Sodium   373.6mg
Carbohydrates   30.3g
Protein   5.9g

Ingredients
4 flour tortillas
8 oz. cream cheese, soft
2 tbsp sugar
1/4 tsp vanilla
1/4 cinnamon
1 apple, sliced
butter
cinnamon-sugar mixture

Directions
1. In a bowl, add the sugar, cream cheese, cinnamon and vanilla and cinnamon beat until creamy.
2. Place the cream cheese mixture onto half of each tortilla, followed by the apples.
3. Carefully, fold each tortilla in half over the filling.
4. In a skillet, add a little butter and cook until melted.
5. Add the quesadillas, 1 at a time and cook
6. until golden brown from both sides.
7. Transfer the quesadillas onto a platter and dust with the cinnamon sugar.
8. Cut each quesadilla into wedges and enjoy.

South
Hollywood Quesadillas

Prep Time: 10 mins
Total Time: 15 mins

Servings per Recipe: 1
Calories	1295.6
Fat	60.2g
Cholesterol	53.5mg
Sodium	2273.1mg
Carbohydrates	159.9g
Protein	40.4g

Ingredients
2 flour 8-inch tortillas
1 medium avocado, peeled, pitted and diced
1 medium mango, peeled, pitted and diced
1/2 C. canned black beans
2 oz. grated Monterey Jack cheese
1/4-1/2 tsp salt
1/4 tsp coriander powder
1/4-1/2 tsp cayenne pepper

lemon juice

Directions
1. In a bowl, add the avocado and drizzle with some lemon juice.
2. In a bowl, add the beans, mango, avocado and seasonings and mix well.
3. Place a lightly greased skillet over medium heat and cook until heated completely.
4. Place 1 tortilla and top with the cheese.
5. Cook until cheese melts completely.
6. Place the beans mixture over the cheese and cover with the remaining tortilla.
7. With a spatula, flip the quesadilla and cook until golden brown.
8. Cut the quesadilla into six wedges and enjoy.

LITTLE CHILI
Quesadillas

Prep Time: 40 mins
Total Time: 1 hr 10 mins

Servings per Recipe: 4
Calories	1218.8
Fat	81.1g
Cholesterol	206.7mg
Sodium	1459.3mg
Carbohydrates	58.6g
Protein	66.4g

Ingredients

3 tbsp olive oil
1 kg beef chuck steak, trimmed of fat, cut into pieces
1 brown onion, chopped
2 garlic cloves, diced
1 red capsicum, diced
3 tsp Mexican chili powder
2 tsp ground cumin
2 tsp dried oregano
1 tsp paprika
800 g diced tomatoes

3 tbsp tomato paste
1 C. water
420 g canned red kidney beans, rinsed, drained
1/2 C. coriander leaves, chopped
4 flour tortillas
1 C. cheese
1 avocado, diced
sour cream

Directions

1. In a pot, add 2 tbsp of the oil over medium-high heat and cook until heated through.
2. Add the beef, capsicum, onion and garlic and stir fry for about 6-8 minutes.
3. Add the oregano, cumin and 2 tsp of the chili powder and stir fry for about 1-2 minutes.
4. Add the kidney beans, tomatoes, tomato paste and water and cook until boiling.
5. Set the heat to low and simmer, covered, for about 19-20 minutes.
6. Meanwhile, for the quesadillas: Place the cheese and remaining chili powder onto 2 tortilla evenly.
7. Cover each with remaining tortillas.
8. In a skillet, add the remaining oil and cook until heated through.
9. Place quesadillas, 1 at a time and cook for about 4 minutes, flipping once half way through.
10. Cut each quesadilla into 8 triangles.
11. Remove the chili con carne from the heat and stir in the coriander, salt and pepper.
12. Enjoy the chili hot with a topping of the avocado and sour cream alongside the quesadilla triangle.

July's
Red Pepper Quesadillas

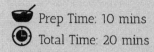 Prep Time: 10 mins

Total Time: 20 mins

Servings per Recipe: 6
Calories	584.5
Fat	24.2g
Cholesterol	35.1mg
Sodium	1449.2mg
Carbohydrates	73.6g
Protein	17.3g

Ingredients

12 tortillas
1 (6 oz.) jars roasted red peppers, drained
and cut into strips
5 1/3 oz. chavrie goat cheese
3 - 4 tbsp butter

Directions

1. Place the cheese onto 6 tortillas evenly, followed by the red peppers strips.
2. Cover with the remaining tortillas.
3. In a nonstick skillet, add the butter and cook until melted.
4. Place the quesadillas, 1 at a time and cook until golden brown from both sides.
5. Cut each quesadilla into 6 wedges and enjoy.

BRAZILIAN
Flank Steak Quesadillas

Prep Time: 20 mins
Total Time: 40 mins

Servings per Recipe: 4
Calories	514.9
Fat	35.1g
Cholesterol	105.8mg
Sodium	457.6mg
Carbohydrates	10.9g
Protein	39.3g

Ingredients
1 lb. flank steaks, cut into strips
chopped garlic
2 tbsp cooking oil
1 lime, juiced
3 tsp Worcestershire sauce
3 tsp liquid smoke
1 large white onion, cut into strips
2 large green bell peppers, cut into strips
2 C. grated cheddar cheese

flour tortilla
guacamole
salsa
salt and pepper

Directions
1. In a bowl, add the garlic, liquid smoke, Worcestershire sauce and lime juice and mix well.
2. Add the steak strips and coat with marinade generously.
3. Refrigerate to marinate for about 25-30 minutes.
4. In a nonstick skillet, add the oil and cook until heated through.
5. Add the bell pepper and onion and cook for about 4-5 minutes.
6. with a slotted spoon, place the onion mixture onto a paper towel-lined plate to drain.
7. Remove the steak strips from the bowl and discard the marinade.
8. In the same skillet, add the steak strips and sear until cooked through.
9. with a slotted spoon, place the steak strips onto a paper towel-lined plate to drain.
10. Divide half of the cheese onto 4 tortillas evenly, followed by the steak, onion mixture and remaining cheese.
11. Cover with the remaining tortillas.
12. Place another nonstick skillet over medium heat until heated through.
13. Place the quesadillas, 1 at a time and cook for about 1-2 minute per side.
14. Enjoy alongside the salsa, pico de gallo and guacamole.

4-Ingredient
Pear Quesadillas

🥣 Prep Time: 5 mins
🕐 Total Time: 10 mins

Servings per Recipe: 2
Calories	185.4
Fat	12.3g
Cholesterol	0.0mg
Sodium	178.0mg
Carbohydrates	16.3g
Protein	3.6g

Ingredients
1 (8 inch) tortillas
1/3 C. shredded Havarti cheese
2 tbsp toasted pecans
pear preserves

Directions
1. Place the Havarti cheese onto one side of tortilla, followed by the pecans.
2. Fold tortilla in half over the filling.
3. Place a greased nonstick skillet over medium-high heat until heated through.
4. Add the quesadilla and cook for about 4 minutes, flipping once half way through.
5. Cut into wedges and enjoy alongside the pear preserves.

HONDURAN
Quesadillas (Egg and Parmesan)

Prep Time: 25 mins
Total Time: 2 h 10 mins

Servings per Recipe: 16

Calories	515 kcal
Fat	23.4 g
Carbohydrates	68g
Protein	9.9 g
Cholesterol	73 mg
Sodium	478 mg

Ingredients
1 1/2 C. margarine
3 C. white sugar
2 C. sifted all-purpose flour
1 C. rice flour
1 tbsp baking powder
6 room-temperature eggs
2 C. lukewarm milk
2 C. grated Parmesan cheese
1/2 C. white sugar

1/4 C. all-purpose flour
1/4 C. sesame seeds

Directions
1. Coat a casserole dish with oil and flour. Then set your oven to 350 degrees before doing anything else.
2. Get a bowl, whisk until fluffy: 3 C. of sugar, and margarine.
3. One by one add in your eggs and keep mixing. Then add: milk, 2 C. flour, baking powder, and rice flour. Mix well. Then mix in parmesan.
4. Get a 2nd bowl, mix: sesame seeds, half a C. of sugar, and one fourth a C. of flour.
5. Layer the first bowl into your casserole dish. Then top with the contents of the 2nd bowl.
6. Cook in the oven for 50 mins. Once finished, cut up the casserole into 12 to 16 pieces. Each piece should be considered quesadilla.

Quesadillas (Steak and Onions)

Prep Time: 10 mins
Total Time: 25 mins

Servings per Recipe: 4	
Calories	552 kcal
Fat	31.1 g
Carbohydrates	40g
Protein	28 g
Cholesterol	79 mg
Sodium	859 mg

Ingredients
2 tbsps vegetable oil, divided
1/2 onion, sliced
1/2 green bell pepper, sliced
salt to taste
4 flour tortillas
1/2 lb cooked steak, cut into 1/4-inch
thick pieces
1 C. shredded Mexican cheese blend

Directions
1. Stir fry your bell peppers and onions for 12 min in 2 tbsps of oil. Coat with some salt before putting everything in a bowl.
2. Coat each of your tortillas with oil on 1 side. Then toast then in the pan on the oiled side.
3. Layer half of each on your tortilla while in the pan: onion mix, steak mix, cheese mix.
4. Place another tortilla on top with it, oiled side facing upwards.
5. Fry this quesadilla for 5 mins per side with a low to medium heat. Place it to the side and cut it in half.
6. Do the same for the other tortilla and the rest of the ingredients.
7. Enjoy.

CHICKEN, BACON
and Mushrooms
Quesadillas

Prep Time: 20 mins
Total Time: 50 mins

Servings per Recipe: 5

Calories	880 kcal
Fat	46.2 g
Carbohydrates	65.6 g
Protein	49.6 g
Cholesterol	121 mg
Sodium	2178 mg

Ingredients

1 lb thinly sliced chicken breast meat
1/2 tsp salt
1/2 tsp ground black pepper
2 tbsps olive oil
14 slices precooked turkey bacon, diced
1 (8 oz.) package sliced fresh mushrooms
1 C. Alfredo sauce
1 tsp butter, or more if needed
5 large flour tortillas

2 C. shredded mozzarella cheese

Directions

1. Stir fry your chicken for 12 mins in oil after seasoning it with pepper and salt.

2. Set aside, remove excess oils from the pan, and julienne your chicken.

3. For 6 mins cook your mushrooms and bacon in the same pan. Then set the heat to low. Add in your Alfredo sauce and chicken. Cook for 3 mins.

4. Get another pan and toast your tortillas in melted butter. On one side of the tortilla add 1/5 of your chicken mushroom mix. Then put 1/5 of your cheese. Fold the other side to form a quesadilla. Cook for 4 mins per side.

5. Repeat for all ingredients. Once everything is done. Cut each quesadilla in half.

6. Enjoy.

Sausage and Chilies Quesadillas

🥣 Prep Time: 15 mins
🕐 Total Time: 40 mins

Servings per Recipe: 4
Calories	598 kcal
Fat	35.9 g
Carbohydrates	47.7g
Protein	22 g
Cholesterol	64 mg
Sodium	967 mg

Ingredients

1 tbsp canola oil
2 smoked beef sausage links, finely minced
1 Poblano chili, finely minced
1/2 red bell pepper, finely minced
1/2 large red onion, finely minced
1/2 C. frozen corn kernels
4 flour tortillas
2 C. shredded Colby cheese

1 tbsp canola oil
1/4 C. sour cream (optional)
1/4 C. salsa (optional)

Directions

1. Cook the following in 1 tbsp of canola for 16 mins: corn, sausage, red onions, Poblano and red peppers.
2. Layer a fourth of the sausage mix on one side of your tortillas. Then fold the other side to make a quesadilla. Do this for all the tortillas.
3. Get a 2nd pan and cook each quesadilla in 1 tbsp of canola for 4 mins per side until the cheese is bubbly.
4. Once all the quesadillas have been cooked cut them in half.
5. Enjoy with a dollop of salsa and sour cream.

VEGETARIAN
Quesadillas

🥣 Prep Time: 10 mins

🕐 Total Time: 20 mins

Servings per Recipe: 5

Calories	389 kcal
Fat	24.5 g
Carbohydrates	31.8g
Protein	14.6 g
Cholesterol	35 mg
Sodium	457 mg

Ingredients

10 (6 inch) corn tortillas
2 C. shredded mozzarella cheese
1 (2 oz.) can sliced black olives
2 avocados - peeled, pitted and sliced
2 tsps hot pepper sauce

Directions

1. Toast your tortilla in a pan for 2 mins per side. Then layer one fourth of your cheese, some avocado, olives, and hot sauce. Top with another tortilla to form a quesadilla.
2. Place a lid on the pan and after 1 min turn it to its opposite side. Place the quesadilla to the side and repeat.
3. Cut the quesadilla in half before serving.
4. Enjoy.

Hannah's
Crawfish Quesadillas

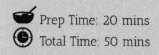 Prep Time: 20 mins

Total Time: 50 mins

Servings per Recipe: 6

Calories	396 kcal
Fat	17.5 g
Carbohydrates	40.1g
Protein	18.9 g
Cholesterol	82 mg
Sodium	628 mg

Ingredients

1 tbsp butter
1 tbsp olive oil
1/2 red bell pepper, minced
4 green onions, sliced thin
1 tbsp fajita seasoning
1/2 tsp cayenne pepper
12 oz. cooked and peeled whole crawfish tails
6 (10 inch) flour tortillas

8 oz. crumbled queso fresco cheese
1 tbsp butter
1 tbsp olive oil

Directions

1. Get a bowl, mix: onions, bell peppers, and fajita seasoning.
2. Cook the mix for 5 mins in 1 tbsp of olive oil and 1 tbsp of butter. Then add your crawfish and cook for about 3 more mins.
3. Layer half of your queso fresco on one side of your tortillas. Then add some crawfish mix, and top with the rest of the cheese. Fold the tortillas in half to form a quesadilla.
4. Get another pan and toast the quesadilla in 1 tbsp of olive oil and 1 tbsp of butter for 4 mins per side.
5. Once finished add more butter and oil to the pan and continue with the remaining ingredients.
6. Enjoy after cutting each quesadilla in half.

MONTEREY CORN
and Beans
Quesadillas

Prep Time: 10 mins
Total Time: 40 mins

Servings per Recipe: 8
Calories	363 kcal
Fat	14.5 g
Carbohydrates	45.6 g
Protein	13.9 g
Cholesterol	26 mg
Sodium	732 mg

Ingredients

2 tsps olive oil
3 tbsps finely diced onion
1 (15.5 oz.) can black beans, drained and rinsed
1 (10 oz.) can whole kernel corn, drained
1 tbsp brown sugar
1/4 C. salsa
1/4 tsp red pepper flakes
2 tbsps butter, divided

8 (8 inch) flour tortillas
1 1/2 C. shredded Monterey Jack cheese, divided

Directions

1. Stir fry your onions for 2 mins in hot oil. Then add in: salsa, beans, red pepper flakes, sugar, and corn. Cook for 4 mins.
2. Get another pan and toast your tortilla in 2 tbsps of melted butter for 1 min. Then layer it with an equal amount of beans and cheese. Put another tortilla on top. Then flip it and let the cheese melt.
3. Repeat with additional butter for all the ingredients.
4. Enjoy.

Southern
Texas Bean Quesadillas

🥣 Prep Time: 15 mins
🕐 Total Time: 45 mins

Servings per Recipe: 12

Calories	504 kcal
Fat	18.3 g
Carbohydrates	69.7g
Protein	14.7 g
Cholesterol	10 mg
Sodium	913 mg

Ingredients
1 tbsp vegetable oil
1 onion, finely minced
2 cloves garlic, minced
1 (15 oz.) can black beans, rinsed and drained
1 green bell pepper, diced
2 tomatoes, diced
1/2 (10 oz.) package frozen corn
12 (12 inch) flour tortillas

1 C. shredded Cheddar cheese
1/4 C. vegetable oil

Directions
1. Stir fry your onions, and garlic until tender in 1 tbsp of oil. Then combine in: corn, beans, tomatoes, and bell pepper.
2. Divide your mix amongst 6 tortillas and top with cheese. Put another tortilla on top of the mix to form a quesadilla.
3. Cook the quesadillas in one fourth of a C. of oil for 2 mins per side or until you find that the cheese is nicely melted.
4. Enjoy.

1ST GRADER'S
Lunch Box Quesadillas

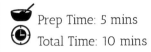 Prep Time: 5 mins

Total Time: 10 mins

Servings per Recipe: 2

Calories	433 kcal
Fat	12 g
Carbohydrates	71.6g
Protein	9.6 g
Cholesterol	16 mg
Sodium	511 mg

Ingredients
4 (8 inch) flour tortilla
2 tbsps softened cream cheese
2 tbsps strawberry jam
1 tbsp confectioners' sugar

Directions
1. Layer the following on each tortilla: 1/2 cream cheese and jam.
2. Put the tortillas on top of each other to make quesadillas.
3. Fry them for 6 mins per side in a pan coated with nonstick spray.
4. Garnish with some confectioner's sugar.
5. Enjoy.

BBQ Tomatoes
and Chicken Quesadillas

🥣 Prep Time: 15 mins
🕐 Total Time: 35 mins

Servings per Recipe: 4
Calories	803 kcal
Fat	29.7 g
Carbohydrates	73.8g
Protein	57 g
Cholesterol	142 mg
Sodium	1536 mg

Ingredients
4 (5 oz.) skinless, boneless chicken breast halves
1/2 C. barbeque sauce
1/3 C. diced fresh parsley
1/4 tsp garlic, finely minced
8 (9 inch) flour tortillas
2 small plum tomatoes, seeded and diced
2 C. shredded Cheddar cheese

Directions
1. Set your oven to 350 degrees before doing anything else.
2. Cook your chicken breast in boiling salted water until fully done. Then remove the water. Shred the chicken into pieces. Then enter it back into the pan. Combine with the chicken: garlic, bbq sauce, and parsley. Stir to evenly coat.
3. Get a casserole dish and put in four tortillas. Layer an equal amount of the following on each: chicken mix, cheddar cheese, tomatoes, and another tortilla.
4. Cook everything in the oven for 8 mins. Then cut them in half before serving.
5. Enjoy.

SOUTHWEST MAYO
for Quesadillas

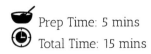

Prep Time: 5 mins
Total Time: 15 mins

Servings per Recipe: 6
Calories	70 kcal
Fat	7.4 g
Carbohydrates	1.1g
Protein	0.2 g
Cholesterol	3 mg
Sodium	149 mg

Ingredients
1/4 C. mayonnaise
2 tsps minced canned jalapeno peppers
2 tsps juice from canned jalapeno peppers
1/2 tsp ground cumin
3/4 tsp sugar
1/2 tsp paprika
1/8 tsp cayenne pepper
1/8 tsp garlic powder
dash salt

Directions
1. Blend or process the following in your chosen appliance for 2 mins: garlic powder, mayo, cayenne, minced jalapenos, paprika, sugar, jalapeno juice, and cumin.
2. Before spreading over tortillas add your preferred amount of salt.
3. Enjoy.

Squash, Mushrooms and Peppers (Vegetarian Quesadillas)

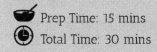 Prep Time: 15 mins

Total Time: 30 mins

Servings per Recipe: 6
Calories	209 kcal
Fat	7.1 g
Carbohydrates	36.8g
Protein	10.2 g
Cholesterol	13 mg
Sodium	441 mg

Ingredients

1/2 C. diced red bell pepper
1/2 C. diced zucchini
1/2 C. diced yellow squash
1/2 C. diced red onion
1/2 C. diced mushrooms
1 tbsp olive oil
cooking spray
6 (9 inch) whole wheat tortillas
1 1/4 C. shredded reduced-fat sharp

Cheddar cheese

Directions

1. For 8 mins cook the following in a pan coated with nonstick spray: mushrooms, red pepper, onions, squash, and zucchini. Set aside.
2. Add more spray to the pan and add in 1 tortilla. Layer the following on it: 1/8 C. cheese, 3/4 C. veggie mix, 1/4 C. cheese, and another tortilla. Repeat.
3. Toast the quesadilla for 4 mins per side. Then dice it into two pieces before serving.
4. Enjoy.

QUESADILLA
Casserole

Prep Time: 15 mins
Total Time: 45 mins

Servings per Recipe: 8	
Calories	493 kcal
Fat	21.2 g
Carbohydrates	50.1g
Protein	26.6 g
Cholesterol	65 mg
Sodium	1423 mg

Ingredients
cooking spray
1 lb ground beef
1/2 C. diced onion
1 (15 oz.) can tomato sauce
1 (15 oz.) can black beans, rinsed and
drained
1 (14.5 oz.) can minced tomatoes with lime
juice and cilantro (such as RO*TEL(R))
1 (8.75 oz.) can whole kernel sweet corn,

drained
1 (4.5 oz.) can diced green chilies, drained
2 tsps chili powder
1 tsp ground cumin
1 tsp minced garlic
1/2 tsp dried oregano
1/2 tsp red pepper flakes
6 flour tortillas
2 C. shredded Cheddar cheese

Directions
1. Coat a casserole dish with nonstick spray. Then set your oven to 350 degrees before doing anything else.
2. Stir fry your onions and beef for 8 mins. Then remove any oil excesses. Add in: red pepper flakes, tomato sauce and minced tomatoes with lime, green chilies, chili powder, corn, oregano, beans, garlic, cilantro, and cumin.
3. Let the mix simmer for 7 mins.
4. Layer the following in your casserole dish: half of the beef, 3 tortillas, more beef, 1 C. cheddar, beef again, more tortillas, beef mix, and finally cheddar.
5. Cook in the oven for 20 mins.
6. Enjoy.

Bacon
and Onions Quesadillas

Prep Time: 15 mins
Total Time: 35 mins

Servings per Recipe: 4
Calories	449 kcal
Fat	21.1 g
Carbohydrates	47.7g
Protein	15.5 g
Cholesterol	37 mg
Sodium	1286 mg

Ingredients
2 tbsps olive oil
1/2 large yellow onion, sliced thin
6 slices turkey bacon, minced
1 tbsp brown sugar
8 (10 inch) flour tortillas
1 C. spicy barbeque sauce
1/4 C. diced fresh cilantro
2 C. shredded Cheddar cheese

Directions
1. Stir fry your onions for 7 mins until tender in 1 tablespoon of olive oil. Then combine in brown sugar, and bacon. Continue frying until the bacon is crispy. Take everything out of the pan.
2. Layer the following on a tortilla: one fourth bbq sauce, 1 tbsp cilantro, 1/4 bacon, half of your cheddar, and 1 tortilla.
3. Cook the quesadilla in a pan for 2 mins per side in 1 tsp of olive oil.
4. Repeat for all ingredients. Then before serving cut the quesadillas in half.
5. Enjoy.

TUSCON QUESADILLA
Dipping Sauce

Prep Time: 10 mins
Total Time: 4 h 10 mins

Servings per Recipe: 18
Calories	93 kcal
Fat	9.8 g
Carbohydrates	1.5g
Protein	0.2 g
Cholesterol	5 mg
Sodium	126 mg

Ingredients
1 C. mayonnaise (such as Hellman's(R))
3 tbsps canned minced jalapeno peppers,
drained (reserve juice)
1 tbsp white sugar
2 tsps paprika
2 tsps ground cumin
1/2 tsp cayenne pepper
1/2 tsp garlic powder
1/4 tsp salt

Directions
1. Get a bowl, mix: salt, mayo, garlic powder, jalapenos, cayenne, 3 tbsps of pepper juice, cumin, paprika, and sugar.
2. Place a lid on the bowl or some plastic wrap and chill in the fridge for 8 hours.
3. Enjoy.

Mediterranean
Goat Cheese Quesadillas

🥣 Prep Time: 15 mins
🕐 Total Time: 40 mins

Servings per Recipe: 4
Calories	346 kcal
Fat	18.5 g
Carbohydrates	33.4g
Protein	11.7 g
Cholesterol	23 mg
Sodium	493 mg

Ingredients
1 onion, diced
6 large cremini mushrooms, diced
2 large cloves garlic, minced
salt and ground black pepper to taste
2 tbsps extra-virgin olive oil
2 tsps balsamic vinegar
1/4 C. herbed goat cheese (chevre)
4 tsps whipped cream cheese
4 flour tortillas

1/3 C. shredded mozzarella cheese

Directions
1. Stir fry in olive oil for 7 mins: mushrooms, black pepper, onions, salt, and garlic, and balsamic vinegar.
2. Get a bowl, mix: goat and cream cheese.
3. Get another pan and toast a tortilla for 2 mins per side.
4. Then layer the following on one side of it: one fourth cheese mix, one fourth mushrooms, one fourth mozzarella.
5. Fold to form a quesadilla. Heat this for 5 mins in the pan. Then repeat for all ingredients.
6. Enjoy.

MEMPHIS HONEY BBQ
Chicken Quesadillas

Prep Time: 20 mins
Total Time: 35 mins

Servings per Recipe: 8
Calories	411 kcal
Fat	14.3 g
Carbohydrates	46.2g
Protein	23.2 g
Cholesterol	48 mg
Sodium	753 mg

Ingredients
2 tbsps vegetable oil, divided
1 onion, sliced into rings
1 tbsp honey
2 skinless, boneless chicken breast halves -
cut into strips
1/2 C. barbeque sauce
1/2 C. shredded sharp Cheddar cheese
1/2 C. shredded Monterey Jack cheese
8 (10 inch) flour tortillas

Directions
1. Set your oven to 350 degrees before doing anything else.
2. Stir fry your onions for 5 mins in 1 tbsp of olive oil. Then add your honey and cook for 1 more min, put the onions in a bowl.
3. Now add your chicken to the pan and also some more oil and cook until fully done. Add in some bbq sauce and stir everything.
4. Layer the following on four tortillas: onions, Monterey, chicken, cheese, and another tortilla.
5. Cook the contents in the oven for 22 mins. Before serving cut them in half.
6. Enjoy.

Cinnamon and Apples
Quesadillas

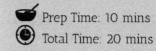 Prep Time: 10 mins

Total Time: 20 mins

Servings per Recipe: 4
Calories	369 kcal
Fat	17.9 g
Carbohydrates	38.4g
Protein	13.8 g
Cholesterol	47 mg
Sodium	652 mg

Ingredients
1 1/2 tsps butter, divided
2 (12 inch) flour tortillas
6 oz. Brie cheese, rind removed and
cheese thinly sliced
1 sweet-tart apple, such as Fugi or Gala,
thinly sliced
1 tbsp brown sugar
1/4 tsp ground cinnamon

Directions
1. Toast 1 tortilla in 3/4 of a tsp of butter.
2. Layer some brie and apple on the tortilla then some cinnamon and sugar, top with another tortilla.
3. Heat everything for 4 mins.
4. Put another 3/4 of a tsp of butter on the tortilla and then turn it over and cook for 4 more mins.
5. Before serving cut the tortillas in half.
6. Enjoy.

CHIPOTLE BASIL
& Tomato
Quesadillas

Prep Time: 10 mins
Total Time: 20 mins

Servings per Recipe: 8
Calories	366 kcal
Fat	20.2 g
Carbohydrates	31.1g
Protein	14.2 g
Cholesterol	38 mg
Sodium	733 mg

Ingredients
8 (8 inch) flour tortillas
2 C. shredded Mexican blend cheese
1 (10 oz.) can minced Tomatoes with
Chipotle
8 slices turkey bacon, cooked and crumbled
1/2 C. diced fresh basil
2 tbsps vegetable oil
Sour cream

Directions
1. One side of each tortilla layer: 1 tbsp of bacon, one fourth C. cheese, 1 tablespoon of basil, 2 tbsps of minced tomatoes.
2. Fold the other side of the tortilla to form a quesadilla. Toast each quesadilla for 2 mins per side in a pan coated with nonstick spray.
3. Repeat this process for all ingredients.
4. Before serving cut the quesadillas in half.
5. Enjoy.

Steak and Onions
Quesadillas

🥣 Prep Time: 10 mins
🕐 Total Time: 45 mins

Servings per Recipe: 4
Calories	927 kcal
Fat	36.4 g
Carbohydrates	101.3g
Protein	46.3 g
Cholesterol	108 mg
Sodium	1985 mg

Ingredients

1 (1 lb) beef top sirloin, thinly sliced
2 small onions, sliced
2 green bell peppers, sliced
1 C. barbeque sauce (such as Bull's-Eye(R)
Texas-Style Bold Barbeque Sauce)
8 (10 inch) flour tortillas
2 C. shredded Cheddar cheese

Directions

1. Set your oven to 425 degrees before doing anything else.
2. Stir fry your beef for 9 mins then add in your bell peppers and onions. Cook for 11 more mins. Then add bbq sauce and stir it for a bit.
3. Let the contents lightly simmer for 12 mins.
4. Get a casserole dish or baking sheet and layer the following on 4 tortillas: beef, cheddar, and another tortilla.
5. Cook everything in the oven for 12 mins.
6. Then turn over each quesadilla and cook for 6 more mins.
7. Enjoy.

GARDEN CILANTRO
and Pepper Quesadillas

🍲 Prep Time: 30 mins
🕐 Total Time: 50 mins

Servings per Recipe: 4
Calories   706 kcal
Fat   35.4 g
Carbohydrates   52g
Protein   46.6 g
Cholesterol   115 mg
Sodium   1301 mg

Ingredients
3 green chili peppers
Pico de Gallo:
1 green bell pepper, halved, divided
2 small tomatoes, minced
1 small onion, divided
3 fresh jalapeno peppers, minced
2 tbsps diced fresh cilantro
2 tbsps tomato juice
1 lime, juiced
1 clove garlic, minced
1/2 tsp salt
1/2 tsp ground black pepper
1/4 tsp garlic salt
Filling:

3 tbsps extra-light olive oil, divided
2 cooked skinless, boneless chicken breast halves, minced
7 mushrooms, sliced
1 tbsp chili powder
1/2 tsp dried oregano
1 pinch garlic salt
1 pinch ground black pepper
1/3 C. red enchilada sauce, or more to taste
Quesadilla:
1/2 C. shredded pepper jack cheese
1/2 C. shredded Cheddar cheese
4 (10 inch) flour tortillas

Directions
1. For 5 mins roast chili peppers under a preheated broiler to get the skins toasted. Once toasted place them in a resealable bag.

2. After setting them aside for 10 mins remove the outside skins from the peppers. Now mince them.

3. Dice half of your onions and bell peppers and then combine them with the following in a bowl: one fourth tsp of garlic salt, one half tsp pepper, tomatoes, salt, jalapenos, garlic, cilantro, lime juice, and tomato juice.

4. Place a lid on the bowl and place the contents in the fridge.

5. Dice the remaining peppers and onions and stir fry them for 7 mins along with mushrooms and chicken in 1 tbsp of olive oil.

6. Combine with the mushrooms and chicken: some black pepper, green chilies, some salt, oregano, and chili powder.

7. Cook for 1 min. Then add in some enchilada sauce.
8. Layer the following on one side of each tortilla: vegetable mix, pepper jack cheese.
9. Then fold it in half to form a quesadilla.
10. Coat the quesadilla with 2 tbsps of olive oil and toast them in a pan for 2 mins per side.
11. Before serving cut the quesadillas in half.
12. Enjoy.

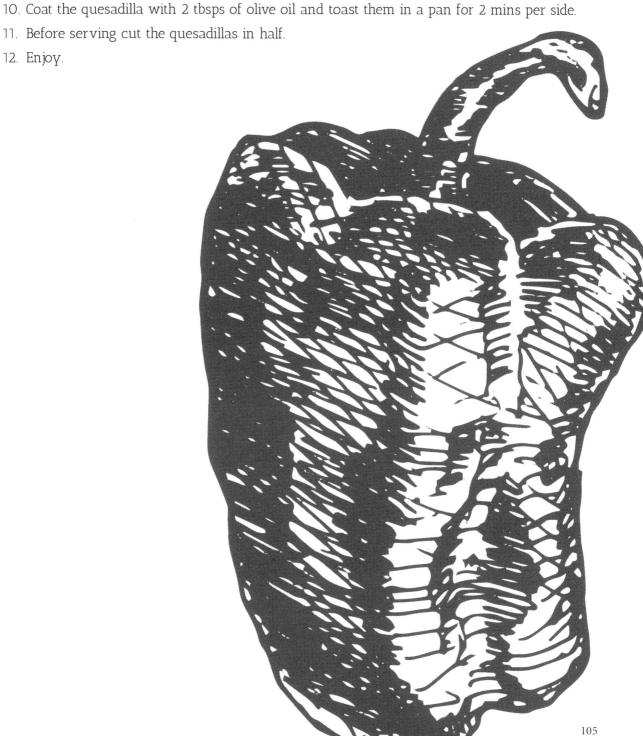

BBQ MONTEREY
Chicken Quesadillas

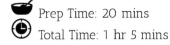

Prep Time: 20 mins
Total Time: 1 hr 5 mins

Servings per Recipe: 4
Calories   481.0
Fat   26.2g
Cholesterol   66.2mg
Sodium   867.2mg
Carbohydrates   43.0g
Protein   19.7g

Ingredients

2 bone-in chicken thighs
1/2 tsp cumin
1 tbsp buffalo seasoning
1 tbsp brown sugar
1/8 C. honey
1/4 C. ketchup
1/8 C. A.1. Original Steak Sauce
1/2 tsp paprika
1/4 tsp garlic powder
1/4 tsp onion powder
1/4 tsp salt
1/4 tsp black pepper

1 tsp prepared mustard
1 tsp red pepper powder
1 tbsp Tabasco sauce
1 tbsp Frank's red hot sauce
1 orange bell pepper, julienned
1/8 C. olive oil
1 medium yellow onion, sliced
1 tbsp granulated sugar
1/4 C. tomatoes, diced
4 oz. Monterey Jack cheese, shredded
2 (10 inch) flour tortillas

Directions

1. Set your oven to 375 degrees F before doing anything else.
2. Cook the chicken in the oven for about 40 minutes.
3. Remove the chicken from the oven and keep aside to cool slightly.
4. In a pot, add the steak sauce, Tabasco sauce, red hot sauce, ketchup, honey, prepared mustard, brown sugar, buffalo seasoning, cumin, paprika, red pepper powder, onion powder, garlic powder, salt, pepper over medium heat and cook until well combined, stirring continuously.
5. Remove from the heat and keep aside.
6. In a skillet add the oil over medium heat and cook until heated.
7. Add the onion, bell pepper and 1 tbsp of the sugar and cook for about 18-20 minutes.
8. Remove from the heat and keep aside.
9. Remove the skin from the chicken and then, shred it.
10. Add the shredded chicken into the sauce and mix until blended nicely.
11. In the bottom of a baking sheet, arrange the tortilla and top with 2 oz. of the cheese, chicken mixture, evenly onion mixture, diced tomatoes and remaining cheese.
12. Cover with the remaining tortilla.
13. Cook in the oven for about 5 minutes.
14. Cut the quesadilla into 8 wedges and enjoy.

Made in United States
Orlando, FL
24 December 2022

27650031R00059